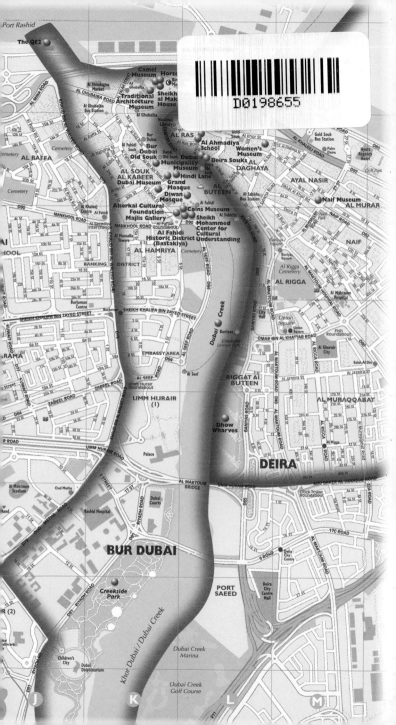

CITYPACK
Dubai

How to Use This Book

KEY TO SYMBOLS	
✚ Map reference to the accompanying fold-out map	🛳 Nearest riverboat or ferry stop
✉ Address	♿ Facilities for visitors with disabilities
☎ Telephone number	❓ Other practical information
🕐 Opening/closing times	▷ Further information
🍴 Restaurant or café	ℹ Tourist information
🚆 Nearest rail station	✋ Admission charges: Expensive (over 75 AED), Moderate (30–75 AED) and Inexpensive (30 AED or less)
🚇 Nearest subway (Metro) station	
🚌 Nearest bus route	

This guide is divided into four sections

● Essential Dubai: An introduction to the city and tips on making the most of your stay.

● Dubai by Area: We've broken the city into five areas, and recommended the best sights, shops, entertainment venues, nightlife and places to eat.

● Where to Stay: The best hotels, whether you're looking for luxury, budget or something in between.

● Need to Know: The info you need to make your trip run smoothly, including getting about by public transport, weather tips, emergency phone numbers and useful websites.

Navigation In the Dubai by Area chapter, we've given each area its own color, which is also used on the locator maps throughout the book and the map on the inside front cover.

Maps The fold-out map with this book is a comprehensive street plan of Dubai. The grid on this fold-out map is the same as the grid on the locator maps within the book. We've given grid references within the book for each sight and listing.

Contents

Introducing Dubai

Just 35 years ago Dubai was a small desert town relying on trade from the Arabian Gulf. But propelled by a go-getting ruling family and buoyed by oil money, it's become the business hub of the Middle East and a tourist hot spot.

The emirate of Dubai is one of seven that make up the United Arab Emirates. It raced into the 21st century with an ambitious plan to attract millions to this sunny corner of the Arabian Peninsula—the result is a glittering metropolis. The city's infectious confidence produced unique projects that stunned the world, including Burj Khalifa, currently the planet's tallest building, and the artificial Palm Islands, so big they can be viewed from space.

Sublime beaches and warm seas were a starting point, but countless dollars have been invested to make Dubai a destination of superlatives. The hotels are the most luxurious; the shopping malls the largest; you can enjoy a gourmet dish for every meal. The nightlife is smoking hot, the spas ultra-cool and the recreation possibilities almost limitless.

The city is amazingly multicultural. Millions of foreigners have settled to make a living, from management-level workers in the hi-tech media and financial sectors to legions of taxi drivers, waiters and housekeeping staff. However, generous Arab hospitality remains a signature of Dubai and the Emiratis who call it home. Yes, you will notice social and cultural differences, but the city has a relatively relaxed attitude to its visitors from around the world.

Dubai is one of those places that polarize opinion: if you don't enjoy a sanitized, somewhat artificial environment or the idea of whiling away hours hunting bargains or chasing a golf ball, Dubai may not be the place for you. But those who appreciate extraordinary architecture, exceptional hospitality and a bewildering choice of recreation will find Dubai delights.

FACTS AND FIGURES

- Population: 1.2 million in 2005; 3 million in 2018—of which around 245,000 are Emiratis
- Visitors: 3 million in 2000; 10.16 million in 2012; 15 million in 2017
- Hotel rooms: 110,000
- Passengers at Dubai International Airport: 88 million in 2017
- Number of shopping malls: 78

THE UNITED ARAB EMIRATES

Dubai is one of seven emirates that together form the United Arab Emirates. The largest—economically and physically—is Abu Dhabi, which takes the lead on military and political matters. The other emirates are Sharjah, Ajman, Umm Al Quwain, Ras Al Khaimah and Fujairah. Each emirate is ruled by a family dynasty. Dubai's rulers are the Al Maktoum family.

SHEIKH MOHAMMED

Born in 1949, Mohammed bin Rashid Al Maktoum was the third son of previous ruler Sheikh Rashid. In his youth he underwent officer training in the UK. He became the head of the Dubai police force in 1968, and the first defence minister in the newly formed United Arab Emirates in 1971. He has been Crown Prince of Dubai since 1995 and ruler since 2006.

EXPAT LIFE

Dubai has enticed foreign businesses by creating ultramodern infrastructure and Free Zones with long-term tax exemptions. White-collar workers enjoy tax-free salaries and perks including housing allowances, health care and free schooling for their children. No surprise then that it's a popular location to build a career or make a new life.

A Short Stay in Dubai

DAY 1

Morning Start the day at **Dubai Museum** (▷ 27), where local Emirati history and lifestyle is brought to life, then explore the **Al Fahidi Historic District** (▷ 24) and shop for souvenirs at **XVA Gallery** (▷ 40).

Mid-morning Stop for a refreshing fruit juice at **Arabian Tea House** (▷ 42). Then take the five-minute *abra* ride across Dubai Creek and build up an appetite with a little haggling at the **Spice or Gold souk** (▷ 50–51).

Lunch Bayt Al Wakeel (▷ 43) on the Bur Dubai side overlooking the creek offers typical local cuisine with a view.

Afternoon Make your way to Sheikh Zayed Road (the Metro is quick but a taxi will be less expensive for a group) and take the lift to the viewing platform at **Burj Khalifa** (▷ 62–63) for awe-inspiring cityscapes.

Mid-afternoon To escape the last of the afternoon heat, head into **The Dubai Mall** (▷ 68–69), currently the largest mall in the world. Do a little shopping or visit the **Dubai Aquarium** (▷ 64).

Dinner Dine around the Middle East at Ewaan (▷ 79) where the open kitchen and buffet offers a range of options. Enjoy views of Burj Khalifa and the Downtown Dubai skyline as you dine.

Evening Stroll down Sheikh Mohammed bin Rashid Boulevard at **Old Town** (▷ 73) in the shadow of Burj Khalifa and watch the evening performance of **The Dubai Fountain** (▷ 65). Finish your evening at **Level 43 Sky Lounge** (▷ 77) at the Four Points Sheraton, currently the world's tallest hotel, with a breathtaking high-rise view of Dubai's bright lights.

DAY 2

Morning Prepare yourself with a generous breakfast. Your tour company will pick you up early for your desert safari in the **Arabian Desert** (▷ 102). Leave the city far behind and head out into the dunes. This is a very different Dubai: it's an action-packed morning of high-adrenaline activities, including buggy dune bashing, sand surfing and camel rides.

Lunch You'll need to recharge after an energetic morning, so head to the relaxed **Bussola on the Beach** (▷ 97–98) for a huge choice of tasty pizzas fired in a wood-burning stove, and a great view of the ocean.

Afternoon Explore the alleyways and waterfront walkways of **Madinat Jumeirah** (▷ 90) with its traditional architecture. Browse the souk and take a boat ride on the canals. You can enjoy close-up views of **Burj Al Arab** (▷ 86), sitting just offshore.

Mid-afternoon If you have an appetite, relax over afternoon tea in the genteel surroundings of the **Al Fayrooz Lounge** (▷ 97).

Dinner Make a reservation at one of Dubai's premier tables to enjoy the Indian dishes created by Michelin-starred chef Vineet Bhatia at **Indego by Vineet** (▷ 98) or, if your budget doesn't stretch to this, **Zataar W Zeit** (▷ 98) in Dubai Marina is a casual café offering great local food.

Evening Take a turn on the **Dubai Eye** (▷ 87), the largest such wheel in the world, and gaze at the glistening towers of Dubai Marina from off-shore, then toast Dubai with a final drink at **Barasti Bar** (▷ 96), where you can enjoy a cocktail and admire the skyline of Palm Jumeirah and Dubai Marina, with your bare feet luxuriating in Dubai's fine sandy beach.

▶ ▶ ▶

Al Ahmadiya School
▷ **48** Dubai's first school, founded in 1912, is now a lesson in history.

Al Fahidi Historic District (Bastakiya) ▷ **24** The historic quarter is full of traditional architecture.

Arabian Desert ▷ **102** A vast sea of dunes and arid plains, just outside Dubai.

Ski Dubai ▷ **91** It's all downhill—on real snow—on the indoor slopes here, on skis, snowboards or bobsleigh.

Shindagha and the Heritage & Diving Villages ▷ **32–33** A living museum in the center of old Dubai, bringing Dubai's traditional ways back to life.

Sheikh Saeed Al Maktoum House ▷ **31** Historic government palace and fine family home.

Sheikh Mohammed Center for Cultural Understanding ▷ **30** Helping forge bridges of friendship with their guided cultural tours.

The QE2 ▷ **29** Iconic ocean liner turned hotel and museum.

Madinat Jumeirah ▷ **90** Arabic-inspired architecture at this modern resort and entertainment complex.

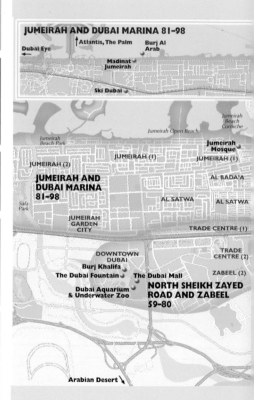

Jumeirah Mosque
▲ ▷ **88–89** Elegant Islamic
▲ place of worship, open to
▲ visitors by guided tour.

Hindi Lane ▷ **28** The spiritual home-from-home for Dubai's large Indian community.

Heritage House ▷ **52** How the wealthy pearl traders of Dubai lived in the early 20th century.

These pages are a quick guide to the Top 25, which are described in more detail later. Here they are listed alphabetically, and the tinted background shows which area they are in.

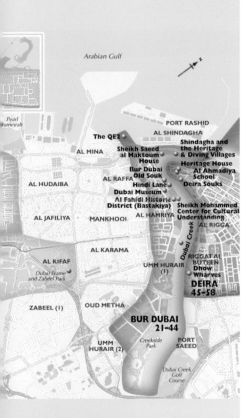

Arabian Gulf

Pearl Jumeirah

PORT RASHID
AL SHINDAGHA
The QE2
Shindagha and the Heritage & Diving Villages
AL MINA
Sheikh Saeed al Maktoum House
AL RAFFA
Heritage House
Al Ahmadiya School
Bur Dubai Old Souk
Hindi Lane
Dubai Museum
Deira Souks
Al Fahidi Historic District (Bastakiya)
Sheikh Mohammed Center for Cultural Understanding
AL HUDAIBA
AL HAMRIYA
AL RIGGA
AL JAFILIYA
MANKHOOL
AL KARAMA
RIGGAT AL BUTEEN
AL KIFAF
UMM HURAIR (1)
Dhow Wharves
Dubai Frame and Zabeel Park
DEIRA 45–58
ZABEEL (1)
OUD METHA
BUR DUBAI 21–44
UMM HURAIR (2)
Creekside Park
PORT SAEED
Dubai Creek Golf Course

Dubai Creek

◀ ◀ ◀

9

Shopping

Dubai is one of the best shopping cities in the world, and attracts an international crowd who flock to buy its high-value items. The city's traditional souks are atmospheric must-see places to explore and shop, but the city has truly embraced the air-conditioned mall—with temperatures topping 100 degrees Fahrenheit in the summer, who wouldn't? The mega-malls The Dubai Mall and Mall of the Emirates are the two stand-out venues.

Perfumes and incense

Arab culture holds scent in high regard and their perfumes are always oil based. Natural oil essences can be applied on the wrist or behind the ear, mixed with base oils for massage, and added to oil burners to scent a room. Perfume shops blend oils and package these unguents in ornate glass vessels that make ideal souvenirs. You'll find lots of different incense, along with incense burners—every Emirati home has several—but frankincense from neighboring Oman is the most prized.

Gold and jewelry

Buyers are attracted to Dubai from around the world for the exceptional prices of gold and jewelry. The price of gold is set by the international markets, but in Dubai jewelers charge less for the craftsmanship used to create the finished jewelry. This is why it's possible to get a bargain—especially in the Gold Souk—though jewelry shops abound.

DUBAI SHOPPING FESTIVAL

Prices across the city are slashed at the month-long sales fiesta during January and millions of dollars are given away in competitions where prizes also include supercars and apartments. A whole host of special events, such as concerts, expand the social calendar. More than 3 million visitors flock to the city to spend, spend, spend during the festival, and hotels in all price ranges are always full, so it pays to reserve ahead.

Clockwise from top: The Gold Souk; the Mall of the Emirates; Bur Dubai Old Souk; Emirates Towers; the Spice Souk

Spices

You'll find sacks piled high with saffron, pepper, turmeric, cloves, nutmeg and chili at the Spice Souk. Buy what you need by weight, or pick up ready-packaged selections of spices.

Arabic handicrafts

From simple copper pots to ornately worked light fittings to hand-blown glass to carved wooden jewelry boxes, there's something for every room in your home.

Persian rugs

Dubai is a major importer of hand-woven Persian carpets, and prices here are lower than, say, London or New York. Most sellers will arrange export for you, so you don't need to worry about baggage allowance on your return flight home.

Designer bliss

If you shop by label, you'll find paradise in Dubai. For high-value designer monikers like Giorgio Armani or Jimmy Choo, the sheer concentration of big names in one place will thrill you. If your budget doesn't quite cover the high price tags, mainstream names such as Bench and Zara also have space here.

Middle-Eastern modern art

Dubai is the hub of a growing market in Middle Eastern art, particularly the work of Emirati and Persian artists. The galleries of the Al Fahidi District make a good place to start but Al Quoz, close to the Mall of the Emirates, is developing into a locally well-known "Arts District."

BUYER BE AWARE

Dubai has a low VAT rate of 5%, so you'd imagine that prices across the board would be cheaper than you'd pay at home. But it's not always so. Prices for designer goods are about the same as in Europe or the US. It pays to do a little research on any high-value items you intend to buy before you travel if you want to grab a bargain.

Shopping by Theme

Department stores, designer boutiques and traditional souks: you'll find them all in Dubai. On this page shops are listed by theme. For a more detailed write-up, see the individual listings in Dubai by Area.

Animal Themes
The Aquarium Store
   (▷ 74)
The Camel Company
   (▷ 74)

Accessories
The Cobbler (▷ 74)
Jafferjees (▷ 40)

Art
Cuadro (▷ 75)
The Empty Quarter
   Fine Art Photography
   (▷ 75)
Gallery One (▷ 75)
Golden Pen Engraving
   (▷ 39)
Majlis Gallery (▷ 36)
Mozaiic Art Gallery
   (▷ 75)
Showcase (▷ 75)
XVA Gallery (▷ 40)

Books
Magrudy's (▷ 95)

Carpets
AGAS Traders (▷ 39)
Heritage Carpets (▷ 75)
National Iranian Carpets
   (▷ 95)

Clothing
Bur Dubai Old Souk
   (▷ 25)
Fabindia (▷ 39)
Giordano (▷ 55)
Hollywood Textiles
   & Tailors (▷ 40)
Khaadi (▷ 55)
Rinco Matching Center
   & Tailoring (▷ 40)
Shaymartian (▷ 95)

Food
Bateel (▷ 39)
The Spice Souk
   (▷ 51)

Gold and Jewelry
Ceylon Master Gems
   (▷ 74)
Chetan (▷ 74)
Damas (▷ 75)
The Gold Souk
   (▷ 50)
Koraba (▷ 55)
Momentum (▷ 75)

Handicrafts
Al Shareif Gallery (▷ 74)
Bab Al Funoon (▷ 39)
D.tales (▷ 95)

Perfumes and *Oudhs*
Abdul Samad Al Qurashi
   (▷ 74)
Ajmal (▷ 55)
Amouage (▷ 39)
The Perfume Souk
   (▷ 50–51)
Swiss Arabian (▷ 55)

Shopping Malls
Al Ghurair Mall (▷ 55)
BurJuman (▷ 39)
Cityland Mall (▷ 106)
Deira City Center (▷ 55)
Deira Night Souk (▷ 55)
The Dubai Mall
   (▷ 68–69, 74)
Dubai Marina Mall
   (▷ 95)
Dubai Outlet Mall
   (▷ 106)
Festival City Mall (▷ 55)
Gold and Diamond Park
   (▷ 74)

Ibn Battuta Mall (▷ 106)
Mall of the Emirates
   (▷ 93, 95)
La Mer (▷ 93)
Reef Mall (▷ 55)
Souk Al Bahar (▷ 74)
Souk Madinat (▷ 90, 95)
Wafi City (▷ 39)
The Walk (▷ 95)

Sporting Goods
Snow Pro (▷ 95)

Souvenirs
Al Jaber Gallery (▷ 95)
Raffles Boutique (▷ 40)
Royal Dirham (▷ 40)

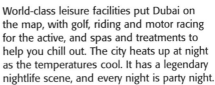

Dubai by Day... and Night

World-class leisure facilities put Dubai on the map, with golf, riding and motor racing for the active, and spas and treatments to help you chill out. The city heats up at night as the temperatures cool. It has a legendary nightlife scene, and every night is party night.

Getting active
Vast tracts of Arabian Desert have been transformed for sporting and leisure pursuits. These are a drive inland from the tourist areas, though usually no more than 30 minutes.

Relax and unwind
Wellness is big business and the best spas are impressive palaces to pleasure, usually found in luxury hotels. Less expensive day spas are located around the city.

Nightlife
Dubai's bars and clubs buzz with a varied and international crowd and it's an ever-changing scene. A listings magazine will help you get the best out of your stay. Emiratis enjoy whiling away the evening at a café with a *shisha* (hookah or water-pipe). Many hotels have fashionable outdoor *shisha* cafés.

Night lights
Dubai is beautiful by night. Traditional architecture in Al Fahidi District, Madinat Jumeirah and Old Town glows, while the towers of north Sheikh Zayed Road and Dubai Marina dazzle. The best places for an evening stroll are along Dubai Creek, around Dubai Marina, and on Sheikh Mohammed bin Rashid Boulevard.

From top: the terrace at Toscana; Souk Madinat Jumeirah; a belly dancer entertaining tourists

RAMADAN

During Ramadan nightlife venues may close, local shops alter their opening times, restaurants may not serve alcohol and hotels may curtail daytime food services during the month-long dawn-to-dusk fast. The three-day Eid Al Fitr festival held at the end of Ramadan is the liveliest holiday of the year for Muslims, with festivities all over the city.

Where to Eat

Though it's a small city, upwardly mobile Dubai has attracted some of the finest culinary talent on the planet and you'll have no trouble filling your trip with outstanding taste sensations from every continent.

Dubai in a nutshell
The restaurant scene tends to revolve around the hotels—given that Dubai has some of the finest hotels in the world, it means quality is high but it also means prices are too.

The world on a plate
The choice is vast; every culinary trend is followed and every regional cuisine has its place. Bistro and gastro pub, sushi bar and steakhouse, rest day brunch and afternoon tea, you can find it all here. Vegetarians are also well catered to, with many Middle Eastern, Asian and Indian restaurants serving delicious meat-free options.

Not just for shopping
The malls have a great range of places to eat, often with more affordable prices. You'll find contemporary and chic eateries here, with a surprising number of famous names.

Opening hours
Some upscale restaurants are open for dinner only—core hours 7–10 but often longer—but many also open for lunch around 11.30 until 3. Many mall restaurants and all cafés are open throughout the day, except during Ramadan (▷ 13).

From top: Hoi An Rest at Shangri La; tasty Fattoush, Tabbouleh and Baba Ghanoush; a dish at Nobu

---

DRESS CODE

In restaurants, smart casual is your guide. This means long pants and a shirt for men and full sandals or shoes (not flip flops). For women most normal summer fashions are acceptable, just nothing too revealing. If you intend to wear something sleeveless or with shoestring straps, carry a shawl or light long-sleeved blouse or cardigan to slip on your shoulders when out and about.

Where to Eat by Cuisine

There are places to eat to suit all tastes and budgets in Dubai. On this page they are listed by cuisine. For a more detailed description of each venue, see Dubai by Area.

American
Claw BBQ (▷ 79)

Asian
Betawi Café (▷ 43)
Blue Elephant (▷ 57)
Creekside Japanese
    Restaurant (▷ 57–58)
Dapoer Kita (▷ 43)
Gypsy (▷ 44)
Hanoi Naturally (▷ 98)
Hoi An (▷ 79)
Karma Kafé (▷ 79)
Katana (▷ 79–80)
The Noodle House
    (▷ 80)

British and Irish
Carter's (▷ 43)
The Irish Village (▷ 58)
Sherlock Holmes Pub
    (▷ 44)

Celebrity Chef
Carluccio's (▷ 79)
Ronda Locatelli (▷ 98)
Todd English Food Hall
    (▷ 80)
ToroToro (▷ 98)

Gourmet
Bateaux Dubai (▷ 43)
Table 9 (▷ 58)

Indian
Amal (▷ 78)
Antique Bazaar (▷ 42)
Aryaas (▷ 43)
Gazebo (▷ 44)
Indego by Vineet (▷ 98)
Mumtaz Mahal (▷ 44)

Mediterranean
Bice (▷ 97)
The Boardwalk (▷ 57)
Bussola on the Beach
    (▷ 97–98)
Casa de Tapas (▷ 57)
Cucina (▷ 58)
Elia (▷ 44)
Da Gama (▷ 58)
Seville's (▷ 44)
Splendido (▷ 98)

Middle Eastern
Abdel Wahab (▷ 78)
Al Hadheerah Arabic
    Evening (▷ 106)
Al Mallah (▷ 42)
Al Mandaloun (▷ 78)
Al Safadi (▷ 57)
Bayt Al Wakeel (▷ 43)
Ewaan (▷ 79)
Local House (▷ 44)
Shabestan (▷ 58)
Zaatar W Zeit (▷ 98)
Zaroob (▷ 80)

Seafood
Divaz (▷ 106)
Seafood Market (▷ 58)
Nathan Outlaw at Al
    Mahara (▷ 98)

South American
Café Habana (▷ 78–79)
Nathan Outlaw at Al
    Mahara (▷ 98)
Taqado Mexican Kitchen
    (▷ 80)

Steak and Grills
The Beach Bar & Grill
    (▷ 97)
Exchange Grill (▷ 79)
The Rib Room (▷ 80)

Tea Houses and Cafés
Al Fayrooz Lounge
    (▷ 97)
Arabian Tea House
    (▷ 42–43)
Choix Patisserie and
    Restaurant (▷ 57)
Dome (▷ 43–44)
La Farine Café and Bakery
    (▷ 79)
Markette (▷ 80)
Morelli's Gelato (▷ 80)

World Cuisine
Al Dawaar (▷ 57)
Fumé (▷ 98)
Spice Island (▷ 58)

Top Tips For...

However you'd like to spend your time in Dubai, these top suggestions should help you tailor your ideal visit. Each sight or listing has a fuller write-up elsewhere in the book.

ANIMAL ENCOUNTERS
Sashay across the dunes on a camel in the Arabian Desert (▷ 102).
Get a peck on the cheek from a sea lion at Sea Lion Point, Atlantis, The Palm (▷ 84–85).
Come face to face with a dolphin at Dubai Dolphinarium in Creekside Park (▷ 34–35).
Spot a pink flamingo on the *sabkha* (salt flat) at Ras Al Khor Wildlife Sanctuary (▷ 73).
March in the snow with the penguins at Ski Dubai (▷ 91).

COCKTAILS AND DANCING UNDER THE STARS
Kick off your shoes and have your feet in the sand at Nasimi Beach at Atlantis, The Palm (▷ 96–97).
Sway with the palm trees to the music at Barasti Bar (▷ 96).
Chill out under the palms on the rooftop pool deck at iKandy at the Shangri-La Hotel (▷ 77).
Arrive by boat to rock that "I'm a film star" look at 101 One&Only The Palm (▷ 96).

ISLAMIC STYLE, THEN AND NOW
Explore the alleyways of old Bastakiya in the Al Fahidi Historic District (▷ 24).
Stroll around Dubai's 21st-century homage to tradition at Old Town, Downtown Dubai (▷ 73).
Window-shop at the theme-parkesque alleyways of Souk Madinat Jumeirah (▷ 90).
Admire the neo-Fatimid monumental porch and minarets of Jumeirah Mosque (▷ 88–89).
Snap a selfie in front of the dhow-inspired curves of Burj Al Arab (▷ 86).
Gaze through the Islamic calligraphy windows of the Museum of the Future (▷ 72–73).

Clockwise from top left: Meeting a dolphin; Raffles Hotel; the Super Suites at the The Palm, Dubai's Gold

ROOMS WITH ATTITUDE

Sleep in ultimate luxury in a duplex suite at the Burj Al Arab (▷ 112).

Enjoy elegance personified in the world's highest building at the Armani Hotel (▷ 112).

Look out from the heart of the glass pyramid at Raffles Dubai (▷ 112).

See the incredible views of Dubai's contemporary skyline from the Shangri-La (▷ 112).

Get inspired for a home makeover at the chic boutique XVA Hotel, where you can peruse and purchase original works as you enjoy breakfast (▷ 109).

Surround yourself with authentic and beautiful Islamic interior design at Orient Guest House (▷ 109).

Step up to the tee amongst the greens at The Address Montgomerie (▷ 110).

CELEBRITY PLATES

Indulge in the savoir-faire of the delicious pastries at Choix Patisserie and Restaurant by Pierre Gagnaire (▷ 57).

Savor the *Cucina Italiana* as inspired by the late Antonio Carluccio at Carluccio's (▷ 79).

Delight in the cultured curry of Vineet Bhatia at Indego by Vineet (▷ 98).

Revel in the zesty, tangy Latin American flavors from Richard Sandoval at ToroToro (▷ 98).

Browse the extensive menu served from 12 open kitchens at the expansive 12,000sq ft Todd English Food Hall (▷ 80).

RETAIL THERAPY

Strut down Fashion Avenue and shop till you drop in The Dubai Mall where you can find all the designer names (▷ 68–69).

Haggle for gold and gems at The Gold Souk (▷ 50).

Stock up the food cupboard at The Spice Souk (▷ 51).

Augment your home decor at the XVA Gallery, Al Fahidi District (▷ 40).

Take your time to select some serious art along Alserkal Avenue (▷ 70).

Souk; a display of decorated perfume bottles; Souk Madinat Jumeirah interior; chilled drinks at the Ikandy UltraBar

SWINGING THE CLUBS

Drive off at the Emirates Golf Club course, home of the Omega Dubai Desert Classic tournament (▷ 96).

Avoid the water hazards at The Address Montgomerie, designed by Colin Montgomerie, winner of eight European Order of Merit tournaments (▷ 106).

Score a hole-in-one at The Els Club course, designed by four-times major winner Ernie Els (▷ 106).

STUFF FOR KIDS

Splash around at Juha's Dhow and Lagoon, Wild Wadi (▷ 94).

Get into a snowball fight at Ski Dubai (▷ 91).

Become an airline pilot for the day at KidZania, The Dubai Mall (▷ 77).

Make some blue buddies at Smurfs Village, Dubai Parks and Resorts (▷ 103).

GETTING YOUR HEART PUMPING

Plunge headlong down a nine-story drop in the Tower of Neptune at Aquaventure Waterpark, Atlantis, The Palm (▷ 84–85).

Take on the black run at Ski Dubai (▷ 91).

Snorkel with the sharks at Dubai Aquarium (▷ 64).

Kick up the sand in a dune buggy in the desert (▷ 102).

SEE FOR MILES

At the slow-turning wheel of Dubai Eye (▷ 87).

Across the Emirate from the terrace of At the Top, Burj Khalifa (▷ 62–63).

From the old city to the contemporary towers from Dubai Frame (▷ 66–67).

BUILD-UP SPEED

Hang from a wire at XLine zipline (▷ 92).

Put your foot down at Dubai Autodrome (▷ 106).

Jump into thin air from an aeroplane with Skydive (▷ 97).

From top: The golf course at Address Montgomerie; kids will love Wild Wadi; Aquaventure Water Park

Dubai by Area

Bur Dubai

On the southern shores of Dubai Creek, Bur Dubai is the old settlement of the Bani Yas, the tribe of the ruling family. Arabic mansions, the city's most authentic heritage attractions and its finest historic district are all here.

Top 25

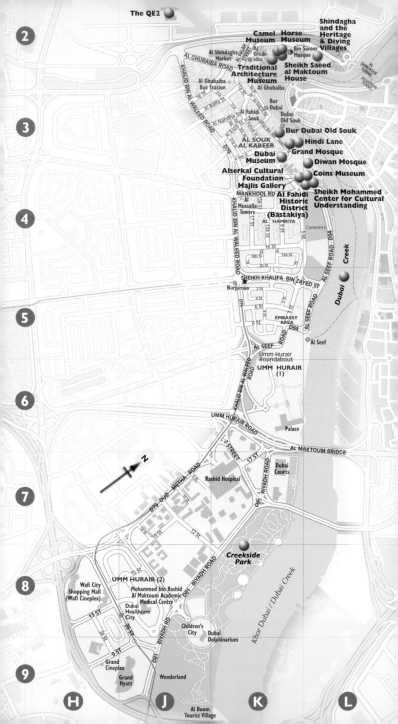

0   500 m
0   500 yds

(M)   (N)   (P)

Al Fahidi Historic District (Bastakiya)

Coffee pots displayed in the sand (left); the district lit up by night (right)

THE BASICS

cultures.ae

🔹 L4

✉ Al Fahidi Street

☎ 353 6666 (Sheikh Mohammed Center for Cultural Understanding)

🍴 Cafés and restaurants ($–$$)

Ⓐ Al Fahidi

♿ Good

🚌 Al Fahidi

HIGHLIGHTS

● Genuine old Arabic architecture
● The biggest group of old *barjeels* in Dubai
● Characterful cafés
● Fascinating galleries

TIP

● The Sheikh Mohammed Center for Cultural Understanding (▷ 30) can organize a guide if required.

Dubai's most complete traditional quarter, Al Fahidi was once an affluent neighborhood of Persian traders. This tangle of narrow alleyways is a great place to immerse yourself in the atmosphere of old Dubai.

Al Bastakiya Al Fahidi is an early example of the shrewd forward thinking of Dubai's rulers: in the late 1800s they granted traders from the city of Bastak in Persia (modern-day Iran) tax concessions and easy relocation, in much the same way as today's government encourages immigration. The traders thrived and built a quarter of impressive mansions on the creekside: Al Bastakiya.

Fall and rise By the 1960s the merchants had moved out, and Al Bastakiya nearly fell victim to the building boom. The eastern parts were demolished to make way for new offices. A visit by Prince Charles and Princess Diana in 1989 may have been its savior. Soon afterward the surviving streets were put under a preservation order and sympathetically renovated. Al Bastakiya was renamed Al Fahidi Historic District in 2012.

Today All the buildings—around 50 in all—are made of coral walls covered with a sand plaster, and feature *barjeels*: wind towers used as an ancient form of air-conditioning. They are art galleries, museums, shops and restaurants—all subtly integrated into the historic surroundings.

Bur Dubai Old Souk

Customers browsing
in the souk (left and
center); colorful
textiles for sale (right)

**One of the original marketplaces of this
erstwhile trading city, the Old Souk—also
known as the Textile Souk—is one of
Dubai's most energetic corners. It's a
sequinned kaleidoscope of color.**

Souk style This wide alleyway was covered
with an arched hardwood roof in the 1990s.
Myriad tiny shops fling open their merchandise-
strewn doors, offering a front-of-house show
worthy of a Moulin Rouge costume call.
Favorites among the local expats are shimmering voiles of gold and silver thread, fashioned
into colorful saris or *kameez*, and pashminas
(these make a useful shoulder-cover). Arabian
kitsch is everywhere, from Sinbad-style ornate
slippers to belly-dancing outfits. The market also
does a fine line in inexpensive mass-produced
items, such as logo-emblazoned T-shirts,
shishas and gilded *ittar* bottles.

Serious business If you're shopping for large
amounts of fabric—perhaps for curtains or business suits—this is the perfect location. You can
purchase complete bolts of cashmere, silk, cotton, calico and chintz and have them shipped
back home. Settle down to some serious nego-
tiations inside the store over an Arabic coffee as
the merchants bring samples for you to peruse.
You can even have a dress or suit made during
your stay—the tailors are extremely skilled and
work fast. Also in the area is Meena Bazaar, a
tight tangle of streets. There's an eclectic mix-
ture of goods here, all at bargain prices.

THE BASICS

➕ K3
✉ Al Fahidi Historic
District
🕐 Sat–Thu 9–1, 4–10,
Fri 4–10
🍴 Restaurants and cafés
nearby ($–$$$)
🚇 Al Fahidi
♿ Few
🛍 Dubai Old Souk

HIGHLIGHTS

● The riot of rainbow hues
● Mass-produced kitsch
souvenirs
● High-quality inexpensive
fabrics sold in any quantity

TIP

● The Textile Souk is where
haggling pays dividends,
especially if you are buying
multiple items.

Dubai Creek

Abra *rides (left); old wooden boats contrast with Dubai's modern buildings (right)*

THE BASICS

- L5
- Numerous cafés and restaurants ($–$$$)
- Few
- *Abra* ride inexpensive

HIGHLIGHTS

- The *abra* ferry trip across the creek
- The Dhow Wharves (▷ 49)
- The constant comings and goings of wooden cargo ships on the water

TIP

- The *abra* crossing is an essential Dubai experience. These narrow boats shoot back and forth from Bur Dubai to Deira, and from them you can see both the modern high-rise glass towers and the wind towers and minarets of old Dubai. For a longer tour, you can rent an *abra* by the hour.

Without the creek, Dubai would not be what it is today. This narrow natural inlet facilitated Dubai's development from desert trading post to modern city. Both aspects of Dubai still exist along its busy banks.

A little piece of history After the Maktoum family settled here in 1833, Dubai slowly prospered. The pearl-fishing industry brought money to the port and the souks (▷ 25 and 50–51) thrived. But it wasn't until the creek was dredged in 1960 and Abu Dhabi struck oil, making Dubai's deep-water port essential for importing drilling equipment, that Dubai truly took off as an economic powerhouse.

Then… You don't have to go far to see what life on the creek was like decades ago. Between Maktoum Bridge and the Sheraton Dubai Creek Hotel, Deira's creek side is awash with wooden dhows (▷ 49), small boats unloading everything from vegetables to TVs.

Now… The creek is lined with towers built in the 1980s and 1990s, many housing government buildings and Dubai's first luxury hotels. On the Bur Dubai bank the gentrified Al Seef district fronts the water's edge. As the creek widens, Creekside Park is visible, with the Dubai Creek Golf & Yacht Club on the opposite bank. Dubai Festival City rises ahead, then the creek curves round to the right and broadens still farther into the Ras Al Khor lagoon.

Dubai Museum

The battlements and tower of the fort (left); museum displays (center and right)

This museum offers a fascinating journey back in time, describing life in the emirate over 5,000 years of settlement, from its trading origins to the oil boom and the current construction fever.

Al Fahidi Fort The museum is housed in a national monument, the diminutive but sturdy Al Fahidi Fort, built in the late 18th century to protect the traders and seafarers living at the mouth of Dubai's creek from invasion. You'll walk through sections re-creating traditional housing, the Dhow Wharves, the souk and the mosque, with mannequins of merchants, boat builders, potters and jewelers.

Traditional Bedouin lifestyle An exhibition on the Bedouin people explains how they used their limited water supply to support their nomadic lifestyle and maintain the health of their camels and sheep, two animal species that were pivotal to the Bedouin's success. Another section throws light on desert ecology and how plants and animals survive average temperatures of 104°F (40°C) in summer and just 4.7 inches (120mm) of rain annually.

Pearl trade Dubai's natural pearls were prized for centuries. The museum shows the rudimentary equipment used at the time when the men would make deep dives with a turtleshell clip on their noses, an 11lb (5kg) stone to pull them down, and a rope looped around their foreheads to guide them back up.

THE BASICS

K3
⊠ Al Fahidi Street
☎ 353 1862
🕐 Sat–Thu 8.30–8.30, Fri 2.30–8.30, during Ramadan Sat–Thu 9–6, Fri 2–5
🚇 Al Fahidi
♿ Good
💵 Inexpensive
🛍 Dubai Old Souk

HIGHLIGHTS

● The pearl-diving gallery
● The gallery on Bedouin lifestyle
● The re-creation of the Dhow Wharves
● The old souk area
● The old fort

Hindi Lane

Items for sale in the busy alleyway of Hindi Lane

THE BASICS

✚ K3

✉ 62 A Street, Al Fahidi Historic District

🍴 Street stalls ($)

🚇 Al Fahidi

♿ None

🏪 Dubai Old Souk

DID YOU KNOW?

The Hindu gods:
● Shiva—The Great God
● Vishnu—maintains order in the universe
● Krishna—embodiment of love
● Ganesh—god of wisdom and new beginnings
● Hanuman—monkey god, symbol of strength and perseverance
● Durga—the Mother Goddess, destroyer of evil, protector of the weak
● Kali—the dark goddess
● Lakshmi—goddess of fortune, prosperity and love
● Sarawasti—goddess of knowledge and the arts
● Rama—symbol of chivalry and virtue

Spiritual home of Dubai's Hindu community, Hindi Lane plays host to the only Hindu Temple complex in Dubai. It's one of the most atmospheric and fragrant streets in the city, packed with stalls selling items for *puja* (Hindu ritual prayer).

What and why Twenty-five percent of Indian expat workers are Hindu, and this narrow alleyway—leading to three simple *mandhirs* (temples) to gods Shiva and Krishna, and Hindu guru Sai Baba—is always thronging with worshipers. A range of items is used during *puja,* and tiny stalls along Hindi Lane supply these in vast quantities. *Pushpam* (flower petals and garlands) decorate the statues in the temples and *dhupa* (incense cones and sticks) are burned to scent the air before the statues of the gods are bathed in milk, honey, or *ghee* (clarified butter) in an act of ritual purification. Apart from *puja* paraphernalia, look out for colorful depictions of the major deities, such as elephant-headed Ganesh or Hanuman the monkey god, homeopathic medicines and delicious street foods.

India and Dubai Ties between India and the UAE go back hundreds of years. Today, Indians make up the largest number of expats, with some families having lived here for several generations. In 2011 it was estimated that these workers sent $6.2 billion (£3.8 billion) back to India to support their extended families.

The QE2 docked at Port Rashid cruise port (left); the Golden Lion pub on board (right)

BUR DUBAI TOP 25

The *Queen Elizabeth 2* is an iconic 20th-century ship which harks back to the glorious era of ocean going transatlantic travel. Flagship of the Cunard line, the vessel was the epitome of style and the last word in speed and found a place in the world's hearts, fondly becoming known as the *QE2*.

A ship is born Designed by James Gardner and built for Cunard by John Brown and Co on the Clyde in Scotland, the *QE2* cost £25 million. The last steam-powered liner to come into service, it was launched by Queen Elizabeth II on September 20, 1967 and departed on its maiden crossing from Southampton to New York in May 1969. The *QE2* spent its summers taking passengers between Europe and America and its winters as a cruise ship. It soon gained a reputation for exceptional service.

Retirement After 39 years at sea, changes to international regulations forced it into retirement. During its service it has traveled more than 6 million miles (9.5 million km), completed over 800 transatlantic crossings and carried 2.5 million passengers

A new life in Dubai In 2008 the *QE2* was bought by a Dubai company and docked at the Port Rashid cruise port, but it wasn't until 2017 that its refurbishment into a floating hotel and heritage attraction began and the new *QE2* officially opened in October 2018.

THE BASICS

qe2.com

☩ J2

✉ Port Rashid

☎ 526 8888

🕐 Heritage tours at 1pm, 3pm, 5pm, 7pm; lounges and bars open throughout the day

🍴 Several restaurants and bars ($$–$$$)

🚇 Al Ghubaiba

♿ Very good

✋ Guided tours expensive

DID YOU KNOW?

● The *QE2* rescued 500 passengers from the fire-stricken French liner *Antilles* in 1971.

● The ship went to war in the Falkland Islands in 1982 as a troop ship.

● The ship ran aground close to Martha's Vineyard in 1992.

● The *QE2* was hit by a 90ft (27m) rogue wave spawned by Hurricane Luis in 1995.

Sheikh Mohammed Center for Cultural Understanding

TOP 25

Cultural tours (left and center); the building's exterior (right)

THE BASICS

cultures.ae

✚ L4

✉ House 26, Al Mussallah Road, Al Fahidi Historic District

☎ 353 6666

🕐 Sun–Thu 8–4, Sat 9–1

🚇 Al Fahidi

♿ Good

🎫 Cultural tours and meals moderate

ℹ Cultural tours: 60-min tours Sun–Thu 9am, 90-minute tours Sun, Tue, Thu 10.30am, Sat 9am; Cultural meals: breakfast Mon, Wed 10am, lunch Sun, Tue 1pm, dinner Tue 7pm; Jumeirah Mosque tour: Sun–Thu 10am

🚊 Al Fahidi

HIGHLIGHTS

● The opportunity to interact with Emiratis in a social atmosphere

● The chance to learn about the Bedouin roots of the Bani Yas tribe

● Exploring the current lifestyle of your Emirati hosts

Founded by the current Sheikh in 1998, the aim of the center is to increase cross-cultural understanding in this diverse and multi-cultural corner of the world, under the motto "Open doors. Open minds."

Cultural tours The center offers several guided tours that will enhance your understanding of Dubai history and Emirati society. You can take a 60-minute or 90-minute tour of Al Fahidi Historic District (old Bastakiya, ▷ 24). Both these tours offer background information about the traditional architecture and the longer tour, includes a visit to the Diwan Mosque (▷ 35).

Cultural meals Enjoy a range of traditional local foods with an informative Emirati host who'll be happy to answer any questions that you have about his Bani Yas tribe, Islam and Emirati lifestyle and customs. Advance reservations are required. You don't need to book to take the Jumeirah Mosque tour (▷ 88–89). Just be at the mosque at 9.45am.

Emirati national dress Men wear a *kandura* (known in Dubai as a *dishdasha*), a full-length, sleeved light coat of white cotton, with a *kaffiyah* (white cotton headdress), held in place by an *agal* (a light rope). Women wear the *abaya*, a long, black, loose-fitting light coat. Their hair is covered with a *hijab* that wraps around their neck. Some women also choose to wear the *niqab* (face veil).

The exterior of the house (left); wind tower (center); detail of a door (right)

Sheikh Saeed Al Maktoum House

This exceptional Arab mansion, the house and *majlis* of former ruler Sheikh Saeed Al Maktoum, is now a museum documenting Dubai's transition from desert state to skyscraper city through a collection of fascinating black-and-white photographs.

Sheikh Saeed Grandfather of the current prince, Saeed ruled from 1912 until his death in 1958. His reign was a challenging time for Dubai, with economic crisis brought on by the collapse of the pearl trade in the 1920s when Japan began to create cultured pearls. He didn't live to see the discovery of oil in the region, dying the year that the fields were confirmed.

The house This is classical Emerati architecture on the grandest scale. Constructed over two stories in 1896 from traditional coral covered in lime and sand plaster, its many rooms are decorated with high-quality rugs and period furniture. *Majlis* means meeting place in Arabic—but Saeed's meetings were much more than a simple get together. This was the epicenter of power during Saeed's reign, where he held court, made decisions and issued edicts.

The collections Two wings of the house display photographs offering fascinating views of Dubai through the last century. The Marine Wing charts the end of the old ways with images of the last pearl divers, while the Al Maktoum Wing shows Dubai's new age.

THE BASICS

➕ K2
✉ Waterfront, Shindagha
☎ 393 7159
🕐 Sat–Thu 8am–8.30pm, Fri 3pm–9pm; during Ramadan Sat–Thu 9–5, Fri 2–5
🚇 Al Ghubaiba
♿ Good
💵 Inexpensive
🚌 Al Ghubaiba

HIGHLIGHTS

● The *majlis*, the meeting room of state
● Exquisite hand-crafted furniture
● Photographs of the pearl-diving community
● Images of a Dubai of yesteryear in the mid to late 1900s

TIP

● Philatelists will love the collections of postage stamps, including those issued by the Trucial States (precursor to the UAE) from 1853 to 1971.

Shindagha and the Heritage & Diving Villages

THE DIVING VILLAGE قرية الـغوص

HIGHLIGHTS

● Being enveloped in the atmosphere of the desert camp
● Your chance to come face-to-face with a camel
● A close encounter with a trained falcon
● Sipping traditional sweet mint tea while sitting around the fire

Immerse yourself in the Dubai of the past and dive into the traditional Bedouin lifestyle of the Arabian Desert without leaving the city, at the most important living museum in the emirate.

The district One of the oldest districts in Dubai, Shindagha became home to the ruling family's Bani Yas tribe when they left their Bedouin lifestyle behind at the beginning of the 20th century.

Bedouin traditions The village itself is set in a huge courtyard. As you enter you'll see a clutch of *barasti* (diminutive thatched huts) that signal the Bedouin village: a faithful interpretation of the desert camp, with real people re-enacting how generations of the Bani Yas lived. Their

The Heritage & Diving Villages in Bur Dubai chart the history of pearl diving, which at one time was the major industry of Dubai

camels wait patiently and sheep lie quietly in their pens. While the women sit weaving and make Arabic sweets, the men are busy metal working or preparing their falcons for the hunt.

Diving for pearls Pearls were the economic lifeblood of Dubai for several generations, but diving to find the valuable gems was dangerous, with men reaching depths of 130ft (40m) with no breathing apparatus. The Diving Village re-creates the Creek waterfront of this era, showing the divers getting ready to set out on a diving trip, mending equipment and their boats.

When to visit Evenings are the best time to visit, as the restaurant serves traditional Emirati dishes and local families come to enjoy the cool air and relax together.

THE BASICS

✚ L2

✉ Shindagha waterfront

☎ 393 5725

🕓 Sun–Thu 8am–10pm, Fri–Sat 3pm–10pm. During Ramadan Sat–Thu 9am–2pm and 8.30pm–midnight, Fri 8.30pm–midnight

🚇 Al Ghubaiba

♿ Few

🖐 Free

🛍 Shindagha

33

More to See

ALSERKAL CULTURAL FOUNDATION

Built in 1925, this traditional Emirati mansion now houses the mission of the Alserkal Cultural Foundation. The main aim of the foundation is the showcasing and promotion of regional arts and culture. An ever-changing program of exhibitions concentrates on Emirati and Gulf-states artists and traditional cultural forms.

➕ K4 ✉ Al Fahidi Historic District ☎ 353 5922 ⏰ Daily 9am–7pm 🚇 Al Fahidi ♿ Few 🎟 Free 🚌 Al Fahidi

CAMEL MUSEUM

Built in the 1940s close to Sheikh Saeed Al Maktoum's house, this building was originally a camel stables. Several rooms are filled with well-presented information about these "ships of the desert". But the most fun exhibit here is the surround-effect re-creation of a camel race, complete with the sound of a crowd and a life-size model you can ride.

➕ K2 ✉ Shindagha ☎ 515 5377 ⏰ Sun–Thu 8–2 🚇 Al Ghubaiba ♿ Few 🎟 Free 🚌 Al Ghubaiba

COINS MUSEUM

This old Al Bastakiya mansion now displays almost 500 rare and valuable coins dating from as far back as the Rashidun Caliphate c. AD 632, minted just after the Prophet Mohammed's death. Other interesting examples come from around the Arab world, including Fatimid, Mamluk and Ottoman examples.

➕ L4 ✉ By Al Farooq Mosque, Al Fahidi Historic District ☎ 392 0093 ⏰ Sun–Thu 8–2 🚇 Al Fahidi ♿ Few 🎟 Free 🚌 Al Fahidi

CREEKSIDE PARK

dubaidolphinarium.ae
At 548 acres (222ha), Creekside is a very large park. A respite from the bustling streets of Bur Dubai, it has something for everyone. The views are sensational, and families will love the open space and entertaining activities. Horticulturalists will

Exhibition in the Alserkal Cultural Foundation

Close-up of an Arabic coin

enjoy themed gardens containing 280 plant species. But the main attraction of Creekside Park is its cable-car system, which runs along a stretch of Dubai Creek shoreline 98ft (30m) above the ground. Children's City is an interactive area for kids aged 2–15, where children can explore the world of nature, space and communications. There's a planetarium with daily shows. Dubai Dolphinarium has dolphin and seal shows, or you can reserve a swim-with-the-dolphin session. There are other rather strange attractions here, including a mind-boggling Mirror Maze and a 5D/7D effects cinema.

✚ K8 ✉ Riyadh Road. There are several gates accessing the park, each with a car park ☎ 336 7633 (Children's City 334 0808, Dubai Dolphinarium 336 9773) ⏰ Park: Sat–Tue, Thu 8am–11pm (Fri 8am–11.30pm women and children only); Children's City: Sat–Thu 9–8, Fri 3–9; Dubai Dolphinarium shows: Mon–Sat 11, 3 and 6 🍴 Snacks from stalls in the park ($) ♿ Good 💰 Park: inexpensive; Children's City: inexpensive; Dubai

Dolphinarium show: moderate ❓ Bicycle rental from Gate 2 for additional fee

DIWAN MOSQUE

Built in 1990 as the mosque for the Diwan or government buildings to which it's attached, the whole complex is Mamluk Islamic in design, in homage to the architectural style developed during the rule of the Mamluk dynasty across the Arab world, c.13th–16th centuries.

✚ L3 ✉ Al Musalla Roundabout, Al Fahidi Historic District 🚇 Al Fahidi ♿ Few 💷 By guided tour only, through the Sheikh Mohammed Center for Cultural Understanding (▷ 30) 🚇 Al Fahidi

GRAND MOSQUE

Dubai's largest mosque hides itself away among the cluster of streets in the heart of the souk district in Bur Dubai. Standing on the site of an original 1900 building, the present mosque dates from the late 1990s and is rather unassuming in design. The Anatolian-style minaret —looking much like a lighthouse

Worshipers in front of the Grand Mosque

tower—is the tallest in the city at 230ft (70m).

➕ K3 ✉ Al Fahidi Historic District ☎ 392 0368 ⊙ Not open to non-Muslims 🍴 Al Fahidi ♿ None 🚇 Dubai Old Souk

HORSE MUSEUM

This small museum explores the importance of the Arabian stallion in the traditional Arab lifestyle. There's a lot here for horse lovers to explore, from the history of the Arabian breed to traditional horse care in the desert.

➕ K2 ✉ Sheikha Mozah bint Saeed House, Shindagha ☎ 515 5379 ⊙ Sun–Thu 8–2 🍴 Al Ghubaiba ♿ Few 🎟 Free 🚇 Al Ghubaiba

MAJLIS GALLERY

themajlisgallery.com

Expat Alison Collins fell in love with Dubai and the traditional architecture of Al Bastakiya. When she arrived, there was little in the way of an arts scene, and the gallery functioned as a meeting place and showcase for the arts community.

Since then, Majlis has developed into one of the premier galleries in the UAE. The building itself is worth a visit, but it's the range of art mediums on show that make it a must for any prospective purchaser.

➕ K4 ✉ Al Musalla Roundabout, Al Fahidi Historic District ☎ 353 6233 ⊙ Jun-Aug Sat-Thu 10am–2pm; Sep–May Sat–Thu 10am–6pm 🍴 Al Fahidi ♿ Good 🎟 Free 🚇 Al Fahidi

TRADITIONAL ARCHITECTURE MUSEUM

Built in 1927 as the home of Sheikh Juma bin Maktoum, this large mansion is a prime example of Islamic and Arabic design. The museum explores and explains traditional Arabic and Islamic design, showing the forms and patterns used by architects. It also displays dioramas of traditional building methods, with mannequins of builders and plasterers at work.

➕ K2 ✉ Shindagha District ☎ 515 5000 ⊙ Sun-Thu 8–2 🍴 Al Ghubaiba ♿ Good 🎟 Free 🚇 Al Ghubaiba

Traditional Architecture Museum

The tallest minaret of the Grand Mosque (opposite); Majlis Gallery (below)

Bur Dubai District

Bur Dubai is one of the oldest neighborhoods in the city and the most rewarding to explore on foot. Its key sights, strung along the creek, bring Dubai's history to life.

DISTANCE: 1.8 miles (3km) **ALLOW:** 5 hours with stops

START

HERITAGE & DIVING VILLAGES 🔲 L2

END

AL FAHIDI HISTORIC DISTRICT (BASTAKIYA) 🔲 L4

① Start from the Heritage & Diving Villages (▷ 32–33) at the mouth of the creek. Explore the re-creation of a traditional Bedouin desert camp and a pearl diving village before moving on.

② Keeping the creek on your left, you walk only a few hundred yards before you see Sheikh Saeed Al Maktoum House (▷ 31) on your right. This is a fine example of traditional architecture with an interesting collection of photographs of old Dubai.

③ Continue to follow the creek around to the left until you reach the Bur Dubai *abra* station. It's always busy with people here. Turn right, then left into the covered alleyway of the Old Souk (▷ 25). Inside the souk you will pass stalls selling clothes, snacks, fabrics and souvenirs.

⑦ At the end of Al Fahidi Street, before the roundabout, you'll arrive in Al Fahidi Historic District (▷ 24). This is the largest area of old traditional architecture in the city. Explore the alleyways and wind towers, browse the Majlis Gallery (▷ 36) and stop for refreshments at Arabian Tea House (▷ 42) next door.

⑥ After exiting the museum, turn left along Al Fahidi Street, crossing a small intersection to join a strip of neon-lit shops.

⑤ Before you pass the mosque turn right, away from the creek and uphill. The Dubai Museum (▷ 27) in the Al Fahidi Fort is ahead. The entrance is on the far side, past a ship used for pearl diving, called a *sambuk*.

④ Continue until you reach the end of the souk and the Grand Mosque (▷ 35), which has the tallest minaret of any mosque in Dubai, at 230ft (70m).

Shopping

BUR DUBAI MALLS

Bur Dubai's main malls are the Egyptian-themed Wafi City (wafi.com) in Oud Metha, and BurJuman (burjuman.com) with its plethora of haute-couture names. Air-conditioned Modern Al Fahidi Souk, close to the historic Bur Dubai Souk, is covered and air conditioned. It sells many similar goods to the traditional souk, but it doesn't have the bustling atmosphere.

AGAS TRADERS

wafi.com

With trading contacts throughout the Gulf and westward to Turkey and the Kurdish region, AGAS offers an excellent collection of handmade rugs and carpets, complemented by a small but high-quality selection of antiques and handicrafts.

🔰 H8 ✉ Murjan Souk, Wafi City Mall, Oud Metha ☎ 327 9780 🕒 Sat–Wed 10–10, Thu–Fri 10am–midnight 🚇 Dubai Healthcare City

AMOUAGE

amouage.com

This upscale store sells *ittars* and blends different oils to produce a range of exclusive off-the-shelf perfumes, as well as bath products and home fragrances.

🔰 H8 ✉ Wafi City Mall, Oud Metha ☎ 324 3135 🕒 Sat–Wed 10am–10pm, Thu–Fri 10am–midnight 🚇 Dubai Healthcare City

BAB AL FUNOON

wafi.com

A small gallery with a fine collection of antiques and handicrafts from around the Arab world. This is not mass-market, but one-of-a-kind pieces—perfect for finding that showpiece holiday souvenir.

🔰 H8 ✉ Murjan Souk, Wafi City Mall, Oud Metha ☎ 327 9727 🕒 Sat–Wed 10–10, Thu–Fri 10am–midnight 🚇 Dubai Healthcare City

BATEEL

bateel.com

Bateel is renowned for its upscale grocery products. Best buys are the dried dates, date cookies and chocolates—all beautifully packaged. There are several outlets around the city.

🔰 K5 ✉ BurJuman Center, Khalid bin al Waleed Road at corner of Trade Center Road ☎ 355 2853 🕒 Sat–Wed 10–10, Thu–Fri 10am–11pm 🚇 BurJuman

FABINDIA

fabindia.com

This is a one-stop-shop for clothing, textiles and homewares produced in India. Almost everything on sale is made by hand using traditional techniques. It's a huge, modern air-conditioned store, which makes it a delight to explore.

🔰 H3 ✉ Nashwan Building, Al Mankhool Road, Mankhool ☎ 398 9633 🕒 Sat–Thu 10–10, Fri 4pm–10pm

GOLDEN PEN ENGRAVING

wafi.com

Islamic calligraphy is an art form, and Amir Hossein Golshani exquisitely engraves or carves it on materials such

DUBAI SUMMER SURPRISES

Younger sibling of Dubai's immense Dubai Shopping Festival discount-fest held during January, Dubai Summer Surprises (summerisdubai.com) is specifically scheduled to pump up visitor numbers during the uncomfortably hot summer season. Running from mid-June to early September, the discounts of up to 75 per-cent have proved a big hit with spenders, who don't need to worry about the outdoor temperatures—they just head to the air-conditioned malls, where it's temperate 24 hours a day all year round.

as wood, leather and stone, and in silver or gold filigree.

🏠 H8 ✉ Murjan Souk, Wafi City Mall, Oud Metha Road ☎ 050 252 2537 🕐 Sat–Wed 10–10, Thu–Fri 10am–midnight 🚇 Dubai Healthcare City

HOLLYWOOD TEXTILES & TAILORS

hollywooduae.com

This long-standing tailors will sell you the fabric, measure you and run you up a suit in 48 hours. They also sell accessories such as ties and cufflinks.

🏠 K3 ✉ 25 C Street, Old Souk, Al Souk Al Kabeer ☎ 352 8551 🕐 Sat–Thu 9.30–1.30 and 4–10, Fri 6pm–9pm 🚇 Al Fahidi

JAFFERJEES

Dubai has many international designer leather goods stores, but Jafferjees is an independent, quality producer with over 125 years of experience with everything from key fobs to luggage.

🏠 K5 ✉ BurJuman Mall ☎ 351 5887 🕐 Sat–Wed 10–10, Thu–Fri 10am–11pm 🚇 BurJuman

RAFFLES BOUTIQUE

raffles.com

Branded items from this upscale hotel chain—towels, bathrobes and clothing, along with a selection of souvenirs from other Raffles locations.

🏠 H8 ✉ Wafi City Mall, Oud Metha ☎ 314 9544 🕐 Sat–Wed 10–10, Thu–Fri 10am–midnight 🚇 Dubai Healthcare City

RINCO MATCHING CENTER & TAILORING

rinco.ae

One of the best places to get your prom or bridal gown made. Take a pattern or a picture and choose the fabric—they have a huge range of finishes and colors. It'll only take a couple of days. They'll also make Indian traditional clothing to your size.

🏠 K3 ✉ Cosmos Lane, Meena Bazaar, Al Souk Al Kabeer ☎ 050 744 9930 🕐 Sat–Thu 9.30am–10.30pm, Fri 4.30pm–10.30pm 🚇 Al Fahidi

ROYAL DIRHAM

Lovers of the kitsch, gauche and garish will adore the selection of mass-market souvenirs and Indian trinkets on sale here, from jewel-encrusted camels to Burj Khalifa miniatures: and all at the lowest prices in the city.

🏠 K4 ✉ Al Musalla Road, Mankhool ☎ 355 4331 🕐 Sat–Thu 10–10, Fri 4.30pm–10pm 🚇 Al Fahidi

XVA GALLERY

xvagallery.com

This gallery/café/hotel is one of the stalwarts of Al Bastakiya, with an inventive program of exhibitions and art on sale. The Design Shop has a huge range of decorative arts, clothing and jewelry. XVA Gallery also has exhibition space at Gate Village in the Financial District close to Sheikh Zayed Road (▷ 71).

🏠 L4 ✉ Al Fahidi Historic District ☎ 353 5383 🕐 Daily 10–6 🚇 Al Fahidi

KARAMA MARKET

For rock-bottom prices on mass-market products like last season's electricals and clothing, head to the alleyways of Karama Market, set around the Al Karama Shopping Center. Be careful though—fake designer items are rife here and the Dubai authorities have periodic crackdowns on importers and sellers. Counterfeit goods can look just like the real thing but they are illegal, so if there are any doubts about authenticity check before you buy.

Entertainment and Nightlife

AHASEES SPA & CLUB

dubai.grand.hyatt.com

A private and relaxing spa with plunge pools, sauna, steam room and Jacuzzi.
J9 ✉ Grand Hyatt Hotel, Umm Hurair (2) ☎ 317 1234 🕐 Daily 9–9 🚇 Dubai Healthcare City, Al Jadef

AL BOOM TOURIST VILLAGE

alboom.ae

Nine dhows set off from Al Boom every evening for cruises down Dubai Creek; prices include onboard dining, with a range of traditional dishes.
J9 ✉ Umm Hurair (2), next to Garhoud Bridge ☎ 324 3000 🕐 Late-night cruises 10.30pm–midnight

AL NASR LEISURELAND

alnasrll.com

An aging complex with a bowling alley, ice-skating rink and tennis and squash courts. Regular upgrades and show events mean its popularity endures.
J7 ✉ Umm Hurair Road, Oud Metha, near the American Hospital ☎ 337 1234 🚇 Oud Metha

BAR BAAR

barbaardxb.com

Popular with the after-work expat crowd and for late-night partying, this large venue has a menu but is more about the vibe than the food.
J4 ✉ Majestic Hotel, Mankhool Road ☎ 55 260 8787 🕐 Daily noon–3am 🚇 Al Fahidi

CLEOPATRA'S SPA

cleopatrasspaandwellness.com

The theme at this spa is ancient Egypt, although the hammam-like wet room has Mediterranean influences. Guests can also access the Pharaoh Club's swimming pool.
H8 ✉ Wafi City, Oud Metha ☎ 324 7700 🕐 Women daily 9–9; men (separate door) Sun, Thu 10–9.30, Fri 10–9 🚇 Dubai Healthcare City

EVE

eveloungedubai.com

A high-rise bar with large terrace and excellent views of the skyline of both old and new Dubai. Relax in the lounge area or sip cocktails at the high-seat bar. DJ sets and live music performances happen regularly.
Off map at H9 ✉ Hyatt Regency Dubai Creek Heights ☎ 553 1214 🕐 Sat–Wed 4.30pm–2am, Thu–Fri 4.30pm–3am 🚇 Oud Metha

KIDS CONNECTION

wafi.com

This huge indoor children's entertainment and activity center puts action at the heart of the fun. This is really the 21st-century air-conditioned version of the old-style playground with swings, see-saws and trampolines, plus electronic games for older children.
H8 ✉ Wafi City, Oud Metha ☎ 327 9011 🕐 Daily 10am–midnight 🚇 Dubai Healthcare City

MAHARLIKI CAFÉ

Popular Filipino café, and nightclub with a weekly program of DJ sets and live

THE BAR SCENE

Dubai's bar scene changes rapidly. Today's hip bar will be tomorrow's has-been, although some places are so swanky they seem to be immune from this syndrome. For the very latest tips on what's hot or not, use an online listings directory such as platinumlist.net or the Wednesday entertainment supplement of the *Gulf News*.

acts. It's a bustling venue with a lively atmosphere.

🞙 K5 ⊠ President Hotel, 101 Sheikh Khalifah bin Zayed Road ☎ 334 6565 🕐 Daily 6pm–2.30am 🚇 Abu Dhabi Commercial Bank (ADCB)

THE PULSE

movenpick-hotels.com
pulsedubai.com

Black leather and stainless steel decor set the scene at this club, which spins a range of house, R&B, hip hop and retro sounds. Women and couples get in free.

🞙 H7 ⊠ Mövenpick Hotel, 19th Street, Oud Metha ☎ 358 2090 🕐 Daily 7pm–3am 🚇 Dubai Healthcare City

VINTAGE WINE BAR

pyramidrestaurantsatwafi.com

A cozy wine bar with an endearing lack of snobbery; the list covers most of the world. Fondue nights are held on Sunday

🞙 H8 ⊠ Pyramids, Wafi City, Oud Metha ☎ 324 4100 🕐 Fri–Wed 6pm–1.30am, Thu 4pm–2am 🚇 Dubai Healthcare City

VOX BURJUMAN

voxcinemas.com

A large multiplex cinema screening mainstream Hollywood and Bollywood films. It also has a specially designed kids' viewing room.

🞙 K5 ⊠ BurJuman Mall ☎ 600 599905 🕐 Daily 8am–10pm 🚇 Burjuman

Where to Eat

AL MALLAH ($)

almallahuae.com

This simple cafeteria-style eatery offers the best *shwarmas* (▷ 58) around. It's a great place to fill up if you are on a budget.

🞙 F4 ⊠ Al Dhiyafa Road, Satwa ☎ 398 4723 🕐 Sat–Thu breakfast; daily lunch, dinner

ANTIQUE BAZAAR ($–$$)

antiquebazaar-dubai.com

One of Dubai's best Indian restaurants, with a devoted Asian clientele, serving excellent food and a comprehensive list of dishes. This is not the best place for a quiet tête-à-tête, though.

🞙 K3 ⊠ Four Points by Sheraton Bur Dubai, Khalid bin Al Waleed Road ☎ 397 7444 🕐 Sat–Thu lunch; daily dinner 🚇 BurJuman

ARABIAN TEA HOUSE ($)

arabianteahouse.co

An essential pit stop on any tour of old Bur Dubai. Super snacks, such as the

ALCOHOL

Many inexpensive restaurants serving expat communities don't have an alcohol license and don't serve alcohol. Instead, you'll be offered delicious fresh fruit juices, a range of international-brand soft drinks, tea (black or green) or infusions such as mint or camomile.

souk salad of couscous, chicken, cashew and lettuce, seem perfectly matched to the tranquil surroundings. The juice bar serves several delicious blends.

⊞ L4 ✉ Al Fahid Street, Al Fahidi Historic District ☎ 353 5071 ⏱ Lunch, dinner Ⓜ Al Fahidi

ARYAAS ($)

aryaasgourmet.com

You'll find some of the best Indian food around at this two-story restaurant. The interior is modern and contemporary but the menu sticks to well-loved staples at an excellent price.

⊞ K5 ✉ Bank Street, opposite BurJuman Mall, Al Hamriya ☎ 357 7800 ⏱ Breakfast, lunch, dinner Ⓜ BurJuman

BATEAUX DUBAI ($$$)

bateauxdubai.com

Contemporary fine dining is only part of the appeal here. The food is excellent but this sleek, modern boat with full-sized glass windows also sets out on a sedate trip along Dubai Creek as you are served with your meal.

⊞ L4 ✉ Dubai Creek, Al Hamriya ☎ 814 5553 ⏱ Dinner Ⓜ Al Ghubaiba

BAYT AL WAKEEL ($)

With a shady terrace jutting out over the waters of Dubai Creek, there's no better place for lunch with a view. The food is authentic and local, with a selection of fresh fish served as you like. Service is variable.

⊞ K2 ✉ Close to Bur Dubai *abra* station, Al Ghubaiba ☎ 353 0530 ⏱ Lunch, dinner Ⓜ Al Ghubaiba

BETAWI CAFÉ ($)

A modern, colorful café serving arguably the best Indonesian food in the city. It's a casual and bustling place, especially in the evenings. The food is delicious.

⊞ J5 ✉ Shop 20–21 Mabrooka 1 Building, Street 4B, Al Karama ☎ 759 8118 ⏱ Breakfast, lunch, dinner (open 24 hours) Ⓜ Abu Dhabi Commercial Bank (ADCB)

CARTER'S ($$)

pyramidsrestaurantsatwafi.com

This modern British-style bar offers a menu based around English pub food. There's an English carvery brunch every Friday and English Premier League games on the big screens.

⊞ H8 ✉ Pyramids, Wafi City, Oud Metha ☎ 324 4100 ⏱ Lunch, dinner Ⓜ Dubai Healthcare City

DAPOER KITA ($)

dapoerkita.com

Dapoer Kita means "our kitchen" in Indonesian, and this basic cafeteria-style eatery is where you'll sit alongside Indonesian expats enjoying excellent authentic dishes.

⊞ H5 ✉ Sheikh Mohammed Building, 43 A Street, Al Karama ☎ 379 5501 ⏱ Lunch, dinner Ⓜ Abu Dhabi Commercial Bank

DOME ($)

domeuae.com

Weary shoppers refuel with coffee, cakes and snacks at this café. Decor is mock-French, with waiters in black-and-white uniforms and dinky berets.

BRUNCH

Brunch on Friday mornings is a Dubai institution. The beginning of the Islamic weekend is the signal for visitors and expatriates to settle down to sumptuous buffets and glasses of chilled champagne at hotel restaurants across the city. The preferred spots are at beachfront hotels, but most hotels will offer some sort of brunch deal.

⊞ K5 ✉ BurJuman Center, Khalid bin Al
Waleed Road at corner of Trade Center Road
☎ 355 6004 🕐 Breakfast, lunch, dinner
🚇 BurJuman

ELIA ($–$$)

dubaimajestic.com

Elia offers Greek food with a modern
twist by celebrity chef Yiannis Baxevanis.
Inventive contemporary dishes match
Mediterranean staples such as Greek
salad and *tzatziki*.

⊞ J4 ✉ Majestic Hotel, Mankhool Road
☎ 501 2666 🕐 Dinner 🚇 Al Fahidi

GAZEBO ($)

gazebo.ae

You can expect great Indian food
combined with excellent service here.
The tandoori-cooked meats are a
specialty, as are the biriyanis and there's
a huge selection of both. You can eat
very well here for less than 80 AED.

⊞ H3 ✉ Kuwait Road, Mankhool ☎ 359
8555 🕐 Lunch, dinner

GYPSY ($–$$)

gypsychinese.com

Gypsy serves up well-produced Chinese
cuisine by a restaurateur who's been in
business since the 1980s. The menu is
extensive and offers a strong selection
of vegetarian dishes.

⊞ J4 ✉ Grand Excelsior Hotel, Kuwait Road,
Mankhool ☎ 653 2004 🕐 Lunch, dinner

LOCAL HOUSE ($)

localhousedubai.com

Delicious Emirati seafood dishes are the
stars of this restaurant but if you're
more in the mood for interesting meat
offerings you can find out what camel
(or kudu and buffalo) tastes like at this
traditional Arabic restaurant. The main
dishes are competitively priced.

⊞ L4 ✉ Al Musalla–Al Fahid roundabout,
Al Fahidi Historic District ☎ 353 2288
🕐 Lunch, dinner 🚇 Al Fahidi

MUMTAZ MAHAL ($)

mumtazmahalrestaurant.com

Mughlai dishes from the northwest of
India are served in a colorful yet refined
dining room. There are several vegetarian and fish dishes, and live music.

⊞ K3 ✉ Arabian Courtyard Hotel, Al Fahidi
Street ☎ 351 9111 🕐 Lunch, dinner
🚇 Al Fahidi

SEVILLE'S ($$)

pyramidsrestaurantsatwafi.com

For entertainment with your tapas, try
Seville's, where a flamenco guitarist
serenades diners. On winter evenings,
as the cocktails flow, the atmosphere
can become positively Andalusian.

⊞ H8 ✉ Pyramids, Wafi City, Oud Metha
☎ 324 4777 🕐 Lunch, dinner 🚇 Dubai
Healthcare City

SHERLOCK HOLMES PUB ($–$$)

arabiancourtyard.com

This is a typical old-style English pub,
serving beer and pies and burgers, with
sport on the TV and regular live bands.

⊞ K3 ✉ Arabian Courtyard Hotel, Al Fahidi
Street ☎ 351 9111 🕐 Lunch, dinner
🚇 Al Fahidi

BUDGET OPTIONS

Follow the legions of blue-collar expat
workers to the Al Karama district for bottom-
dollar, no frills, but ultra-authentic Lebanese,
Emirati, Indian, Thai and Indonesian eateries.
They'll often be quiet early in the evening
but, as the clock races toward midnight, the
tables will be packed with a buzzing crowd.
Don't expect to pay by credit card—these
places usually operate on a cash-only basis.

Deira

North of Dubai Creek, Deira is a densely populated old commercial quarter, bigger on bustle and atmosphere than pretty views. Close to the creek mouth you'll find a cluster of attractions, including some of the most vibrant and economically buoyant souks in the Middle East.

Deira Islands

N (compass)

Hyatt Regency Hotel

Gulf Park

103 ROAD

D85

AL KHALEEJ ROAD

MURAR

4 St

18 St

20 St

D82

NAIF ROAD

OMAR BIN AL KHATTAB ROAD

4 St

10b St

D88

2 St

4 St

6 St

10 St

11 St

Baraha St

15 Street

13 St

CORNICHE DEIRA

Al Baraha Hospital

Kuwait Hospital

21a Street

AL BARAHA

AL KHALEEJ ROAD

Waterfront Market - Fish, Meat, Fruit & Vegetable Market

Al Mamzar Beach Park →

D92

New Dubai Hospital

Baraha St

14 St

16 St

ABU BAKER AL SIDDIQUE ROAD

D78

BIN AL KHATTAB ROAD

AL RASHEED ROAD

15 Street

9 St

24 St

17 St

19a St

18a St

16a St

10b St

85 St

80 St

DEIRA

9 St

22b St

19b St

26a St

24 St

18 St

18a St

24 St

21 St

29 St

20 St

28b St

22c St

28c St

AL RASHEED ROAD

24 St

18 St

29 St

26 St

31 St

37a St

AL MUTEENA

AL MATEENA STREET

D78

Salah Al Din

Reef Mall

13 St

17a St

21a St

A QQABAT

23a St

27a St

29a St

31a St

35 St

37 St

14 St

65a St

SALAHUDDIN ROAD

ABU BAKER AL SIDDIQUE ROAD

AL SIDDIQUE ROAD

Road

0   500 m
0   500 yds

N   **P**

Al Ahmadiya School

TOP 25

Decorated arches (left); a classroom (center); the courtyard (right)

THE BASICS

- L3
- 28 Sikka Street
- 226 0286
- Sat–Thu 8–7.30, Fri 2.30–7.30; during Ramadan Sat–Thu 9–4.30, Fri 2.30–4.30
- Al Ras
- Poor; steps to upper floor
- Free
- Deira Old Souk

HIGHLIGHTS

- Authentic dioramas of 1920s schooling as it used to be
- Photos of the Al Maktoum family through the generations

TIP

- Combine a visit to Al Ahmadiya School with neighboring Heritage House (▷ 52).

Dubai's first school, Al Ahmadiya catered to the children of the elite. Even rulers studied in these simple classrooms: Sheikh Rashid bin Saeed Al Maktoum, Prince of Dubai from 1958 to 1990, was educated here.

The birth of the education system The school first opened in 1912, funded by Sheikh Mohammed bin Ahmed bin Dalmouk, a wealthy pearl merchant. The initial phase consisted of a single story, set round an open courtyard. Demand soon outstripped capacity, so the upper floor and *barjeel* were added between 1920 and 1922. At its peak, occupancy rose to 300 pupils but by 1963 the number of students had outgrown its premises and they were relocated. The school was renovated in 1995 and has undergone another program of redevelopment in the run-up to Expo 2020. Life-size models occupy desks in the formal classrooms where calligraphy, mathematics, literature and astronomy were taught, and sit cross-legged around the Al Muttawa, or religious teacher, learning the Koran by rote.

Education in the UAE Even as the first oil was being pumped out of the desert, the Emirates had no structured education system. There were just 20 schools across the country, catering to around 4,000 students—all boys. When the UAE was formed in 1971, one of its first acts was to formalize education and create a compulsory system through ages 4 to 17.

Traditional wooden dhows (left and center); men loading cargo (right)

Dhow Wharves

Dubai Creek was once one long wharf where dhows would moor up and unload their cargoes. Today only a short section remains, but it's a lively location that provides a snapshot of the past.

When is a dhow not a dhow? Technically the boats that land their cargoes here today are not dhows (Arabic sail boats)—the square-hulled vessels that line up here are all motorized. Still, their wooden hulls and decks hark back to days gone by, having changed little in decades.

Navigating where? Trade from the dhow wharves is mostly bound for local ports. Most of the workaday vessels make short hops across to Iran, around the peninsula to Oman and Yemen, or down the coast of the Indian sub-continent, with a nine- or ten-day turnaround in Dubai for unloading and loading—by hand. It's an amazing insight into how much of this industry is still low tech and labor intensive.

On the deck This is not an area set up as a tourist attraction. With small cranes and lifting equipment constantly on the move, you'll need to pay attention. But it's a gritty, real location where you can chat with crews who love English soccer and like to practice their English.

Watch this space A new development project, Aladdin City—with designs based on the traditional Arabian Nights stories—is planned to sit atop the Dhow Wharves.

THE BASICS

➕ L6

✉ Deira Waterfront, accessed from Baniyas Road

♿ None

🚌 Baniyas

HIGHLIGHTS

● The old-style wooden vessels

● Old working practices long lost at mechanized container ports

● The amazing range of products heading into and out of the city

● Insight into a side of Dubai not normally on the tourist radar

TIPS

● If venturing onto the wharves, wear comfortable shoes and dress modestly.

● A friendly hello ("as-salamu alaykum" in Arabic) breaks the ice.

Deira Souks

DID YOU KNOW?

● Oil-based *ittars* don't contain alcohol like modern western perfumes.
● One drop is enough to perfume your body.
● Body heat intensifies the scent.
● *Ittar* lasts 10 times longer than alcohol-based perfume, can be stored for years and doesn't degrade.

TIPS

● Haggling is compulsory if you don't want to overpay.
● In the evening, the Gold Souk is a great place for people-watching.

Deira's street markets forged Dubai's reputation as an international trading post, selling high-value goods from around the region. Today, little appears to have changed.

The Gold Souk The Gold Souk grew up in the 1940s and this lattice of streets is today lined with more than 300 shops selling gold jewelry. Endless window displays shimmer with millions of dollars-worth of precious metal. And if you don't like any of the bling on offer, a craftsman can create a piece in a couple of days.

The Perfume Souk The shops of the Perfume Souk are known for their range of *ittars*. These are perfume oils produced from natural sources such as flowers or herbs, and can be used

Clockwise from left: Transporting goods in Deira; dried foodstuffs and spices in the Spice Souk; masses of jewelry on sale in the Gold Souk; carrying a rug

singly or blended. You can even create your own unique fragrance. You'll also find incense in its natural forms—rock, crystal, wood and resin—or processed in cones and sticks.

The Spice Souk Goods aren't limited to spices: peppercorns, cinnamon, cloves and nutmeg are in abundance, but you'll also find frankincense, camomile tea, rose petals, dried chilies and lemons. The best buys are vanilla pods and saffron.

The Covered Souk What would have at one time been Deira's main general market is now a riot of mundane but essential items, from pots and pans to brooms and dustpans. Perhaps not a place to shop for souvenirs but certainly a chance to see a slice of everyday life, Dubai-style.

THE BASICS

✚ L3

✉ Spice Souk: Al Ras waterfront; Perfume Souk: off Balidiya Street; Gold Souk: Al Khor Street

🕐 All souks Sat–Thu 9–1, 4–10, Fri 4–10

🚇 Al Ras

♿ Good

🛳 Deira Old Souk

Heritage House

Dioramas in the Heritage House

THE BASICS

⊞ L3
✉ 28 Sikka Street
☎ 226 0286
🕐 Sat–Thu 8–7.30,
Fri 2.30–7.30; during
Ramadan Sat–Thu 9–5,
Fri 2–5
🚇 Al Ras
♿ Poor; steps to upper
floor
👛 Free
🛍 Deira Old Souk

HIGHLIGHTS

● The women's *majlis*
● The shaded *barasti* in the
courtyard
● The clay water-storage
jars and other kitchenalia

Explore how Dubai's well-to-do residents lived in the last century; room by room, Heritage House explains everyday life in a typical family home between 1890 and the 1950s, before the arrival of domestic electricity in the 1960s.

History It was built in 1890 by Mattar bin Saeed bin Muzaaina and was bought by pearl trader Sheikh Mohammed bin Ahmed bin Dalmouk (who funded Al Ahmadiya School) in 1910. It passed into the hands of Ibrahim Al Said Abdullah in the 1930s before the Dubai government, recognizing its value as a window on an era only just vanished, bought and renovated it in the 1990s.

How to explore The house is set over two floors with an outside courtyard, with each room presented exactly as it would have been when in use as a family home. Life-size models depict typical activities. The museum ranks as the most informative in Dubai, with interesting displays and detailed panels.

The heart of the family home The *majlis* is the heart of an Emirati house. It's the room for receiving visitors and, since hospitable Arab families welcomed friends and strangers alike, it is usually separate from the living quarters. Women had their own *majlis* where they could entertain female guests—a display in the Heritage House shows the household's women sewing and applying henna to their hair.

AL MAMZAR BEACH PARK

In an urbanized area, the 222-acre (90ha) Al Mamzar Beach Park is a pleasant open space offering four beaches and several green swaths of land, chalets, barbecue and picnic areas, and playgrounds. The beach areas have changing facilities and sunbeds, and you can rent jet skis to zip through the deeper waters away from the swimming zones. If you'd rather not bathe in the sea, the park has swimming pools with lifeguards on duty, or you can take a trip around on a rented bike or enjoy a ride on a little-train (very popular with families). The large amphitheater hosts regular events, and there are fields for sports including athletics and basketball, plus activity areas for children. You can also rent a chalet for the day.

➕ Off map at P4 ✉ Deira Corniche beyond Al Himriya Port ☎ 296 6201 🕐 Sun–Wed 8am–10pm, Thu–Sat 8am–11pm 👍 Excellent 💷 Inexpensive, swimming pool inexpensive

DEIRA ISLANDS

nakheel.com

The plans for Palm Deira were announced at the height of Dubai's building frenzy, an offshore island like Palm Jumeirah (▷ 94), reaching 7.5 miles (12.5km) into the gulf. Then came the 2008 world financial crisis and the project was put on hold. It wasn't until 2013 that developers Nakheel announced a revamped plan under the name Deira Islands, and the cranes and construction equipment started work again. Deira Islands covers an impressive 5.9sq miles (15.3sq km) with 24.8 miles (40km) of coastline. The residential developments and hotels will be opening through 2019 and 2020. The first attraction to come on line is the Deira Islands Night Souk, with over 5,000 shops along with restaurants and cafés in a waterside setting, which offer competition for Dubai's indoor mega malls.

➕ N2 ✉ Off Deira Corniche 🚇 Palm Deira

Al Mamzar Beach Park

DUBAI MUNICIPALITY MUSEUM

Built in 1957 to house the offices of Dubai Municipality, the building also operated as a classic *khan* or *han*, with commercial premises set below a dormitory for traders who arrived by sea to service the souks. Today the lower floor houses several shops selling tourist souvenirs, while the upper floors display artifacts relating to the development of the city.

➕ L3 ✉ Baniyas Road, on Dubai Creek ☎ 225 3312 🕐 Sun–Thu 8–2 🚇 Al Ras ♿ Few 🎟 Free 🚌 Deira Old Souk

NAIF MUSEUM

Naif Fort was in a sense the changing of the guard in terms of Dubai's architecture. Constructed in 1939 during the reign of Sheikh Rashid as the first HQ of the Dubai Police Force and jail, its first tower section was in the classical defensive style. Restored in the 1990s, it's now a museum relating to the history of Dubai law enforcement. The first police chief was the current Sheikh, who took on the role at the age of 19. Other exhibits include old uniforms and weapons.

➕ M3 ✉ Sikkat Al Khail Road, Naif ☎ 227 6484 🕐 Sun–Thu 8am–2pm ♿ Good 🎟 Free

WOMEN'S MUSEUM

womenmuseumuae.com

This small museum and cultural center offers a glimpse into the lives of women across the UAE. It highlights the various roles played by women to increase cross cultural understanding and acts as a national archive to celebrate female achievement. The galleries offer a showroom space to female artists and have an ever-changing program. There's also a room dedicated to the legacy of poet Ousha bint Khalifa, known as The Girl of the Arabs.

➕ L3 ✉ Sikka 28, off Al Soor Street ☎ 234 2342 🕐 Sat–Thu 10–7 🍴 Banat Bu Ghanem Café ($) 🚇 Al Ras ♿ Good 🎟 Inexpensive

Interior exhibit in the Women's Museum

Shopping

DEIRA MALLS

The north bank of the creek has two large malls. Deira City Center (deiracitycenter.com) is the oldest large mall but it's still a shopping mainstay. Festival City Mall (dubaifestivalcity.com) is beautifully designed. Closer to the heart of downtown is Reef Mall (reefmall.com) and newly renovated Al Ghurair Mall (alghuraircentre.com). There are neighborhood malls in every district. Deira Islands Night Souk is the largest of its kind in the world and opened in 2019.

AJMAL

ajmalperfume.com

Founded in 1951, Ajmal now has over 300 fragrances on its portfolio and supplies concentrated *ittars* (oils) and *eau-de-parfums* in beautiful bottles. It also has exceptional Oudh oil—the most expensive oil in the world.

L8 ⊠ Deira City Center Mall, Baniyas Road, Port Saeed ☎ 295 3580 Sat–Wed 10am–midnight, Thu–Fri 10am–1am Deira City Center

GIORDANO

giordano.com

Selling simple, easy-to-wear fashions, this chain, founded in Hong Kong in 1971, now has stores all across the Asia Pacific region and here in Dubai. Choose from cotton slacks, shirts, jeans and T-shirts, all at reasonable prices.

N5 ⊠ Reef Mall, Salahuddin Road, Al Muraqqabat ☎ 551 903150 Sat–Wed 10am–11pm, Thu–Fri 10am–midnight Salahuddin

KHAADI

khaadi.com

A Pakistani brand which offers elegant women's wear for a great budget. The colorful tops and pants are fashionable and contemporary yet modest, making the perfect clothing for your exploration of the Gulf states.

L8 ⊠ Deira City Center Mall ☎ 423 63403 Daily 10–10 Deira City Center

KORABA

koraba.com

A fine jewelers based in Dubai with a large selection of items in gold, and a gem-studded range. Their specialty, however, is high-quality amber pieces, with resin imported from Poland. Other stores can be found around the city.

Off map ⊠ Festival City Mall, Dubai Festival City ☎ 435 5655 Sun–Wed 10–10, Thu–Sat 10am–midnight

SWISS ARABIAN

swissarabian.com

A Gulf-based company who work with Swiss perfumers to produce a wide range of fragrances in concentrated oil or lighter sprays.

L8 ⊠ Reef Mall, Salahuddin Road, Al Muraqqabat ☎ 526 073847 Sat–Wed 10am–11pm, Thu–Fri 10am–midnight Salahuddin

DUBAI DUTY FREE

Dubai International Airport's duty-free shopping (dubaidutyfree.com) consistently wins accolades as the best in the world. The company posted annual sales of $1.8 billion in 2013, so the customers certainly think so. Not necessarily famed for its knockdown prices, it's the range of goods that make it a winner, plus the fantastic promotions, with prizes including supercars or Dubai property. If you find you've forgotten presents for loved ones back home, you'll be sure to find something here before you leave.

Entertainment and Nightlife

AEROGULF SERVICES

aerogulfservices.com

Get an unparalleled bird's-eye view of Dubai on a (pricey) helicopter tour.
➕ Off map ✉ Dubai International Services, Garhoud Road, Garhoud ☎ 877 6120 🕐 Reservations required

BALLOON ADVENTURES EMIRATES

ballooning.ae

This company's large balloons can carry up to 40 people and be reserved for groups or individuals. Flights take off in time for the sunrise.
➕ Off map ✉ Pick-up from your hotel or from meeting place at the IKEA/Plug In car park at Dubai Festival City ☎ 440 9827 🕐 Oct–May daily

HIBIKI KARAOKE LOUNGE

dubai.hyatt.regency.com

With over 10,000 songs to choose from, there's sure to be something to suit your style. Resident singer Pocholo performs to warm up the audience.
➕ M3 ✉ The Galleria, Hyatt Regency Hotel, D85 Deira Corniche ☎ 209 1234 🕐 Mon–Sat 7.30pm–3am

ICE-SKATING RINK

dubai.hyatt.regency.com

There are regular sessions on the ice here, or lessons are available. You can hire skates, but you'll need to bring socks or buy some at the rink.
➕ M3 ✉ The Galleria, Hyatt Regency Hotel, D85 Deira Corniche ☎ 209 1234 🕐 Mon–Sat 10–12.30, 1–3.30, 4–6.30, 7–10; Sun 10–12.30, 1–4.30, 5–9.30

IFLY

theplaymania.com/ifly

Learn to skydive indoors at this fun attraction where you balance belly-down on a column of air, just a couple of feet off the ground. Tuition for first-timers is included in the price. Ifly also has a virtual skydiving experience, iFLY 2.0, where you don't actually have to leave the ground to enjoy the adrenaline rush of falling through the air.
➕ Off map ✉ City Center Mall, Mirdif ☎ 231 6292 🕐 Sun–Wed 10am–11pm, Thu–Sat 10am–midnight 🚇 Deira City Center

MAKATI COMEDY AND SING ALONG BAR

asianahoteldubai.com

Popular with the growing Pinoy and Pinay expat population from the Philippines, this is one of the few venues in the city to see or perform stand-up.
➕ N5 ✉ Asiana Hotel, Salahuddin Road, Al Muraqqabat ☎ 238 7777 🕐 Mon–Sat 7pm–3am 🚇 Salahuddin

VOX CINEMAS

voxcinemas.com

This multi-screen complex has a newly installed 4DX system, including the effects of rain, fog, wind and lightning to enhance the experience.
➕ L8 ✉ Deira City Center Mall, Baniyas Road, Port Saeed ☎ 600 599905 🚇 Deira City Center

ALCOHOL

You'll notice that all Dubai's bars and clubs are in hotel complexes. This is because these are the only places licensed to sell alcohol. Dubai treads a thin line between welcoming Western tourists and their boozy habits and respecting the Islamic tenets of abstinence. There are a few ground rules. Do not consume alcohol in the streets or behave drunkenly outside nightspots. Once inside a bar, you will find all forms of alcohol widely available.

Where to Eat

PRICES

Prices are approximate, based on a
3-course meal for one person.
$$$ over 300 AED
$$ 150–300 AED
$ under 150 AED

AL DAWAAR ($$–$$$)

hyattrestaurants.com

This is Dubai's only revolving restaurant,
but don't just visit here for the gimmick,
the food served at the international
buffet is high quality, with a vast selection of dishes and cooking stations.
➕ M3 ✉ Hyatt Regency Dubai, Al Khaleej
Road ☎ 209 6914 ⏰ Lunch and dinner
🚇 Palm Deira

AL SAFADI ($–$$)

alsafadi.ae

In this huge courtyard complex with
outside dining and an air-conditioned
dining room you'll find well-cooked,
delicious and uncomplicated Lebanese
and local dishes.
➕ M6 ✉ Al Rigga Road, Al Muraqqabat
☎ 227 9922 ⏰ Lunch, dinner 🚇 Al Rigga

BLUE ELEPHANT ($–$$)

blueelephant.com

A long-standing favorite, this Thai
restaurant has elaborate traditional
decor—you cross a bridge over a carp
pond to get to your table—and the food
works well, with a menu of well-chosen
dishes.
➕ M8 ✉ Al Bustan Rotana Hotel, Casablanca
Road, Garhoud ☎ 282 0000 ⏰ Lunch,
dinner. Closed lunch Sun

THE BOARDWALK ($$)

dubaigolf.com

The Boardwalk offers Mediterranean-
style dishes in an idyllic setting on the
creek with downtown vistas. The deck is
a wonderful place for lunch, but this
place comes alive in the evening.
➕ L8 ✉ Dubai Creek Golf & Yacht Club,
Garhoud ☎ 295 6000 ⏰ Lunch, dinner;
breakfast Fri–Sat

CASA DE TAPAS ($)

casadetapas.ae

This funky bar is an excellent place for
Spanish tapas, with a good choice of
hot and cold varieties for snacks or meal
building. They also serve tasty portions
of paella.
➕ L8 ✉ Dubai Creek Golf & Yacht Club,
Garhoud ☎ 416 1800 ⏰ Lunch, dinner

CHOIX PATISSERIE AND RESTAURANT ($–$$)

diningdfc.com

A little touch of French *je ne sais quoi*
here at Michelin-starred chef Pierre
Gagnaire's venue, where you can stop
for delicious pastries and coffee during
your shopping trip, or explore the full
dinner menu.
➕ Off map at L6 ✉ Dubai Festival City
☎ 701 1136 ⏰ Breakfast, lunch, dinner

CREEKSIDE JAPANESE RESTAURANT ($–$$)

creeksidejapaneserestaurant.com

There's a full range of Japanese cuisine
at this smart café, with cooking stations

CENTURY VILLAGE

Century Village (centuryvillage.ae) is a large
al fresco restaurant complex behind the
Aviation Club in Garhoud. There are nine
venues to choose from, including Da Gama
(▷ 58), with menus from India to Japan to
Italy. As the tables fill up around the huge
terrace there's a great atmosphere. It's a
popular place for the weekend crowd.

each serving up fresh and tasty sushi, noodle and teppanyaki dishes.

🏙 L5 ✉ Sheraton Dubai Creek Hotel and Towers, Baniyas Road, Riggat Al Buteen ☎ 207 1750 🕐 Dinner 🚇 Union

CUCINA ($–$$)

marriott.com

Delightful Italian trattoria with authentic styling and mouth-watering pizzas cooked in a wood-burning stove, along with fresh, tasty pastas and to-die-for risottos.

🏙 N6 ✉ JW Marriott Hotel, Abu Bakr Al Siddique Road, Al Khabaisi ☎ 607 7588 🕐 Lunch, dinner 🚇 Abu Bakr Al Siddique

DA GAMA ($$)

Named after the Portuguese explorer Vasco da Gama, you'll find a selection of this country's favorite recipes, as well as a choice of Mexican dishes.

🏙 M9 ✉ Century Village, The Aviation Club, Garhoud ☎ 282 3636 🕐 Lunch, dinner 🚇 GGICO (Gulf General Investment Company)

THE IRISH VILLAGE ($–$$)

theirishvillage.com

For over 20 years, the best in Irish hospitality and hearty food, of the burgers, pasta and grills variety, has been served up here, and it isn't just the Irish expats who return time after time.

🏙 L9 ✉ Off 2nd Street, Garhoud ☎ 239 5000 🕐 Lunch, dinner 🚇 GCICO

SEAFOOD MARKET ($$–$$$)

seafoodmarket-dubai.com

Set out like a market stall, this is a simple concept. Choose your fish or seafood from the selection on display and the chef will cook it as you like.

🏙 M9, off map ✉ Le Meridien Dubai, Garhoud ☎ 702 2455 🕐 Lunch, dinner 🚇 Airport Terminal 3

SHABESTAN ($$)

radissonblu.com

Iranian restaurant Shabestan serves aromatic breads, kebabs and other Persian classics. Live music adds to the Arabic experience, and the interior has a lavish sultan's palace theme.

🏙 L4 ✉ Radisson Blu Hotel, Deira Creek, Baniyas Road ☎ 205 7033 🕐 Lunch, dinner

SPICE ISLAND ($$)

ihg.com

Multiple cooking stations offer a trip around the world at this all-you-can-eat buffet. It's particularly busy at Friday brunch. There are over 200 dishes to choose from so it's ideal for families.

🏙 N6 ✉ Crowne Plaza Hotel, Salahuddin Road, Al Muteena ☎ 608 8085 🕐 Breakfast, lunch, dinner 🚇 Salah Al Din

TABLE 9 ($$$)

table9dubai.com

One of the Middle East's most innovative dining concepts, the team here create original and ever-changing menus. The six-course vegetarian tasting menu is a rate treat of upscale well-balanced dishes that complement each other.

🏙 L6 ✉ Hilton Dubai Creek, Baniyas Road, Riggat Al Buteen ☎ 212 7560 🕐 Dinner 🚇 Al Rigga

THE *SHWARMA*

The *shwarma* is the fast-food of choice in Dubai and in the downtown districts of Deira and Bur Dubai you'll find stall after stall selling this delicious street food. Thin slices are carved from cooked meat rotating on a rotisserie and this is packed into flatbread with salad and hummus, and the whole thing tightly wrapped in paper. Pick these up to quash the hunger pangs for around 30 AED.

North Sheikh Zayed Road and Zabeel

The modern city first burst out of its confines at the top of Sheikh Zayed Road, the main artery leading south toward Abu Dhabi. Today, this strip is business central, and it offers the emirate's most striking architecture, coolest hotels and classiest dining, shopping and entertainment options.

Top 25

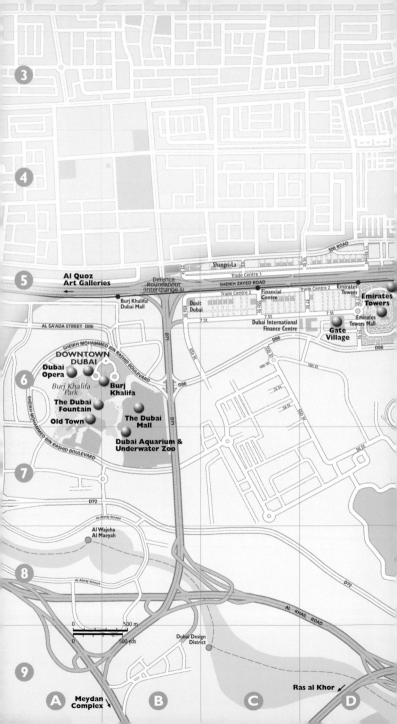

3

4

Al Quoz
Art Galleries

5
Defence
Roundabout
(Interchange 1)

SHEIKH ZAYED ROAD

Shangri-La

Trade Centre 1

Trade Centre 2

Trade Centre 2

Financial
Centre

Emirates
Towers

**Emirates
Towers**

Burj Khalifa/
Dubai Mall

AL SA'ADA STREET D06

Dusit
Dubai

7 St

Dubai International
Finance Centre

Emirates
Towers Mall

SHEIKH MOHAMMED BIN RASHID BOULEVARD

**DOWNTOWN
DUBAI**

Gate
Village

**Dubai
Opera**

*Burj Khalifa
Park*

**Burj
Khalifa**

6

**The Dubai
Fountain**

Old Town

**The Dubai
Mall**

SHEIKH MOHAMMED BIN RASHID BOULEVARD

**Dubai Aquarium &
Underwater Zoo**

7

D72

Al Abraj Street

Al Wajeha
Al Maeyah

8
Al Abraj Street

AL KHAIL ROAD

D72

0   500 m
0   500 yds

Dubai Design
District

9

A   Meydan
Complex ↙

B

C

Ras al Khor ↗

D

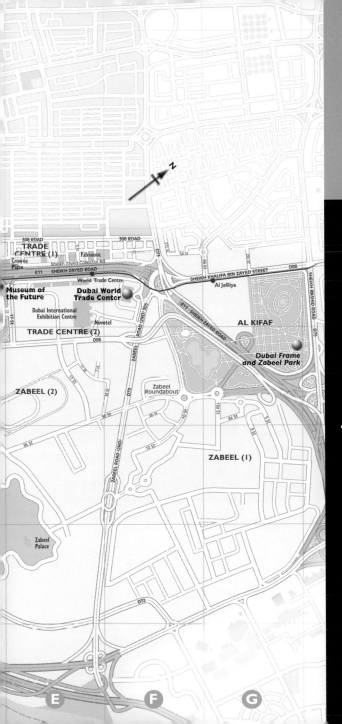

308 ROAD
TRADE
CENTRE (1)
Crowne
Plaza
Fairmont
Sheikh Zayed Collector Rd
E11 SHEIKH ZAYED ROAD
World Trade Centre
308 ROAD

SHEIKH KHALIFA BIN ZAYED STREET
D88
Al Jafiliya

SHEIKH RASHID ROAD
D75

Museum of
the Future
Dubai World
Trade Center
Dubai International
Exhibition Centre
Novotel
TRADE CENTRE (2)
D86

E11 SHEIKH ZAYED ROAD

AL KIFAF

Dubai Frame
and Zabeel Park

ZABEEL (2)

ZABEEL ROAD (2ND)
D73

Zabeel
Roundabout

ZABEEL (1)

Zabeel
Palace

ZABEEL ROAD (2ND)

D72

E

F

G

Burj Khalifa

DID YOU KNOW?

Burj Khalifa holds the following world records:
● Tallest building
● Tallest freestanding structure
● Highest number of stories
● Highest occupied floor
● Highest outdoor observation deck
● Longest elevator flight

The tallest building in the world shoots arrow-like 2,716ft (825m) into the sky above Dubai, a graceful needle of aluminum and glass. It's the most astounding structure in the city, and perhaps the world.

Planning Architect Adrian Smith found inspiration for the Y-shaped base of the tower in a desert flower's petals. The triple-lobed shape helps resist the region's strong winds, while an outer layer of reflective panels withstands the ferocious heat of the Dubai summer.

The community Burj Khalifa was not simply meant to be an impressive status symbol; it was designed as a vertical community. There are 900 apartments serviced by fitness centers and

Clockwise from top left: The Top Sky Lounge; sunlight glistens off the Burj Khalifa; sunset at the Burj Khalifa; people enjoy the sunset at Level 125

swimming pools, shops and a library, and even an 27-acre (11ha) garden. Visitors are no less pampered, with a luxury boutique hotel designed by Giorgio Armani (▷ 112) with eight restaurants and a 12,000sq ft (1,100sq m) spa.

At The Top The operators of Burj Khalifa have installed an amazing visitor attraction offering an exhilarating adrenaline rush and truly jaw-dropping views whatever the time of day. At The Top observation deck sits 124 stories above the ground, and as soon as the elevator door opens you'll be assaulted by 360° uninterrupted views all across Dubai. For a VIP experience (at extra cost), At The Top SKY is 24 stories higher and your own Burj Khalifa "ambassador" will accompany you on a personal tour of what is currently the world's highest public access space.

THE BASICS

burjkhalifa.ae

➕ B6

✉ Near Interchange 1, Sheikh Zayed Road. Entrance to At The Top from basement level in The Dubai Mall (▷ 68)

☎ 888 8124 or in Dubai 800 2884 3867 (800 AT THE TOP)

🕐 At The Top daily 10–10

🍴 On-site restaurants, cafés, bars, At The Top Sky Café

🚇 Burj Khalifa/Dubai Mall

♿ Excellent

🎫 At The Top expensive

❓ Audio guide inexpensive

Dubai Aquarium & Underwater Zoo

Lionfish (left); an observation tunnel (right)

THE BASICS

thedubaiaquarium.com

⊞ B7

✉ Ground Floor, The Dubai Mall, Financial Center Road, off Sheikh Zayed Road

☎ 342 2993

🕐 Daily 10am–2am (ticket office closes 1am)

🚇 Burj Khalifa/Dubai Mall

♿ Very good

🎟 Various ticket packages available starting moderate

HIGHLIGHTS

● The feeling that you're part of the ocean world
● All those sharp teeth at shark feeding time
● King Croc

TIP

● You can have your underwater experiences recorded on film at extra cost.

The towering acrylic walls of this huge 10-million liter tank create an interface between our world of air and the world of water. It's as if a slice of the ocean has been teleported here.

Vital stats Over 140 species, including more than 300 sharks and rays, glide around the space which is 167ft (51m) long, 66ft (20m) wide and 36ft (11m) high. A walk through the acrylic tunnel gives you a surround-sensation effect as they swim over the top of you. The daily feeding sessions up the action, with scuba-clad aquarium staff feeding by hand. The rays get fed at 10.30am and the sharks at 2pm.

Experiences There are several "experiences" to add on to the basic trip. The glass-bottom boat ride is the most sedate, but cage snorkeling and the shark walk—in the cage wearing an oxygenized helmet—put you right at the heart of the action. Spending the day with a keeper and feeding the sharks and other fish with a qualified staff member are also on offer.

Not just sea life King Croc is a 40-year-old saltwater crocodile from Queensland, Australia. He's already over 16ft (5m) in length and weighs 1,600lb (750kg) and is considered one of the biggest captive crocodiles in the world—and he hasn't finished growing! Another gallery re-creates nighttime in the desert wadis and dunes, showing a selection of Dubai's nocturnal animals you'd probably never see otherwise.

The dancing fountains of Burj Khalifa are a popular draw

The world's largest dancing fountain show has been wildly popular since it first broke water in 2009. Thousands of people take a lakeside seat every day for its shimmering performances.

Water The design has a 900ft (275m) long thread of jets, supplemented by five circles, just under 1,500 water jets in all, along with 1,000 fog jets. During the performance, 22,000 gallons (83,000 liters) of water becomes airborne, and the jets of water shoot 500ft (150m) into the air—the height of a 50-story building.

Music and lights But water is only part of the whole. Some 6,600 "superlights" and 25 color projectors create 1.5 million lumens of light formulated into over 1,000 abstract creations. The beams can be seen over 20 miles (32km) away. And of course there's the music. There's a varied repertoire, including the specially penned piece *Sama Dubai*. Others include the haunting *Time to Say Goodbye (Con te partiro)* sung by Andrea Bocelli, *Baba Yetu*, an award-winning song in Swahili, and an Arabic dance track, *Shik Shak Shok*. For the closest views of the evening dancing shows, take a trip onto the lake on an electrically powered *abra*. The ticket office is at the waterfront promenade of The Dubai Mall.

WET California-based WET is the world leader in this field and created the fountains at the Bellagio and Mirage on the Vegas strip, and the fountains at the Olympic Park in Sochi in 2014.

THE BASICS

dubaimall.com
✛ A6
✉ Burj Khalifa Lake, Downtown Dubai
☎ Inquiries through The Dubai Mall 800 38244 6255 (800 Dubai-Mall)
🕐 Sat–Thu 1pm–1.30pm and 6pm–midnight every 30 minutes, Fri 1.30pm–2pm and 6pm–midnight every 30 minutes.
🚇 Burj Khalifa/Dubai Mall
♿ Very good
💧 Free, *abra* ride moderate

TIPS

Best vantage points:
● The promenade walk around the lake
● The bridge between The Dubai Mall and Souk Al Bahar
● The outdoor terrace at Café Madeleine or Joe's Café
● Long-distance view from At The Top in Burj Khalifa

Dubai Frame and Zabeel Park

● Dubai Frame stands 492ft (150m) tall and 305ft (93m) wide, with a bridge connecting the verticals.

● A 269sq ft (25sq m) glass floor atop the structure allows you to look down directly below, while walking on the bridge between the two uprights.

HIGHLIGHTS

● Contrasting view of old and new Dubai
● The scale and proportions

Could it be the world's largest picture frame? In a city of superlatives, why not? Dubai Frame is exactly that—the colossal, beautifully decorated border to some of Dubai's most spectacular townscapes.

Great views Dubai Frame is designed as a cultural attraction which offers a fascinating insight into how Dubai started and how it views its future. During daylight the gold and turquoise Arabic-inspired detail shimmers in the sunlight, but at night Dubai Frame dazzles with color, making it a spectacular sight. Views from the sky-deck level of Dubai Frame are designed to offer contrasts with old Dubai to the north and the towers of the new city to the south.

What's inside Dubai Frame plays host to three fascinating "discovery"' galleries about Dubai:

Clockwise from top left: The Dubai Frame interior at night; one of the interior galleries within the Frame; daytime views of the city

Old Dubai, Present Dubai and Future Dubai. Interesting period footage bring traditions alive once again, while the state-of-the-art computer graphics are effectively employed to show how Dubai hopes to develop over the medium to long term.

Zabeel Park Surrounding Dubai Frame is a planned 116-acre (47ha) green respite from Downtown Dubai. Described as a technology-based recreation area, there are three themed zones featuring interactive exhibits, plus an egg-shaped 2,000-capacity Megabowl amphitheater, Stargate Dubai children's amusement park and a 3D cinema. It's also the venue for Dubai Garden Glow (dubaigarden glow.com), an evening event where 10 million bulbs create some amazing and supremely colorful displays.

The Dubai Mall

HIGHLIGHTS

● The combination of activities
● Fashion Avenue for the concentration of big names
● The lakefront promenade with views of Burj Khalifa and The Dubai Fountain
● Over 80 child-centric role-play activities at KidZania (▷ 77)

TIP

● The mall rents lockers to store your purchases while you continue shopping.

Shopping heaven or shopping hell, The Dubai Mall has over 10.7 million sq ft (1 million sq m) of air-conditioned retail space with more than 1,300 stores. It's the biggest combined shopping and entertainment complex on earth.

Fashion Avenue It's hard to know where to begin, but if you want to prioritize haute couture brands, make your way straight to Fashion Avenue, on the east side of the mall overlooking the lake, where the latest season's offerings by Louboutin, Hermès and Lagerfeld, among others, are there to tempt you.

DubaiDino The Dubai Mall's newest attraction is the skeleton of a *Diplodocus longus*, a dinosaur discovered in Wyoming, USA, in 2008.

The Dubai Mall is biggest shopping mall in the world—make sure you wear your comfortable shoes

Dubai's "dino" is 80ft (24m) long and 25ft (7.6m) high and it would have weighed the same as five elephants.

More than a mall There's plenty to do other than just shop. The entrance and ticket office to the two viewing platforms in Burj Khalifa (▷ 62–63) are on the lower ground floors and Dubai Aquarium (▷ 64) is built into the fabric of the mall. Young visitors will love KidZania (▷ 77) and the ice-skating rink, and entertainment for the whole family is on-screen at the cinema complex. There are plenty of places to eat, from fine dining to snacks, including a selection set along the waterfront promenade with views of Burj Khalifa and overlooking the lake for front-row seats for The Dubai Fountain show (▷ 65).

THE BASICS

thedubaimall.com

🕂 B6

✉ Financial Center Road, off Sheikh Zayed Road

☎ 800 38244 6255 (800 Dubai-Mall)

🕐 Daily 10am–midnight

🍴 Many options

🚇 Burj Khalifa/Dubai Mall

♿ Excellent

More to See

AL QUOZ ART GALLERIES

alserkalavenue.ae

Lying equidistance between Burj Khalifa (▷ 62–63) and Mall of the Emirates (▷ 93), Al Quoz is a small district of low-rise commercial properties that, over the last 20 years or so, has seen the impromptu rise of an urban arts center. It's somewhat of an anomaly in a city where just about every community is planned, but more than 20 galleries and organizations can be found around the nucleus of Alserkal Avenue.

🔢 Off map at A5 ☒ 8th Street, Al Quoz District ☎ 416 1900 🅰 Few/good

DOWNTOWN DUBAI

mydowntowndubai.com

One of Sheikh Mohammed's pet projects, this vast planned community was designed to emulate the spirit of old Dubai, and to develop the Sheikh Zayed Road area beyond its role as a business and convention district. The community motto is "The Center of Now." which rings true—it acts as a magnet for visitors, with the flagship Burj Khalifa (▷ 62–63), The Dubai Fountain (▷ 65), The Dubai Mall (▷ 68–69), Dubai Opera (▷ 70) and Old Town (▷ 73) all sitting within its boundaries, plus Sheikh Mohammed bin Rashid Boulevard encircling the district, with its shopping and dining opportunities, street fairs and festivals.

🔢 A6 ☒ Sheikh Mohammed bin Rashid Boulevard, off Financial Center Road ☎ Customer Center 367 3333 🚇 Burj Khalifa/Dubai Mall 🅰 Excellent 🚌 Boulevard bus tour inexpensive

DUBAI OPERA

Dubaiopera.com

Now the major venue for live entertainment in the city, the 2,000-seat Dubai Opera has far more than opera in its program including major international stand-up comedians, pop artists and classical orchestras. Designed by Atkins group as a tribute to the maritime history of Dubai melded with the birth of the modern city,

Inteior of the Ayyam Gallery

Exterior of Dubai Opera at night

the distinctive curve of the lobby space looks like the prow of a ship.
🔲 A6 ✉ Downtown Dubai ☎ 440 8888 🕙 Tours daily, reservations essential; back-stage tours one day per month, see schedule. Shows as per program 🍴 Dubai Opera Café ($–$$) Ⓜ Dubai Mall ♿ Very good 💷 Tours and tickets expensive

DUBAI WORLD TRADE CENTER

dwtc.com

See where Dubai's transformation from desert trading outpost to home of world-class skyscrapers really kicked off, at the city's first tower. The Dubai World Trade Center has a single, but significant, claim to fame. This honeycombed structure, 488ft (149m) tall, was Dubai's first skyscraper when it was completed in 1979.
🔲 F5 ✉ Trade Center Roundabout ☎ 332 1000 Ⓜ World Trade Center ♿ Good

EMIRATES TOWERS

jumeirah.com

These futuristic twin towers were the first of Dubai's skyscrapers to test the boundaries of what could be created. The contrast with the Dubai World Trade Center couldn't be greater: The city's first skyscraper retains a certain 1970s charm, but the Emirates Towers' piercing apexes symbolized Dubai's drive to succeed.
🔲 D5 ✉ Sheikh Zayed Road ☎ Hotel 330 0000 🍴 Restaurants and bars in the Jumeirah Emirates Towers hotel, and cafés in the Boulevard mall ♿ Excellent Ⓜ Emirates Towers

GATE VILLAGE

difc.ae

Dubai International Financial Center is one of the city's major Free Zones, a planned community cater-ing to the financial services sector. Characterized by a series of dull high-rise towers, the district is domi-nated by The Gate, a distinctive Gensler-designed 15-story glass-sided arch. Gate Village is the social hub of the financial district, with a range of shopping and dining establishments. This is a

Emirates Towers

The Gate, Dubai
International Finance Center

burgeoning center for the arts, with over a dozen high-end galleries and regular arts-related events. Visit the Opera Gallery (operagallery.com), which displays works by Chagall, Miró, Picasso and Rodin.

🔼 D5 ✉ 7th Street, off Sheikh Zayed Road ☎ International Financial Center admin: 362 2222 🚇 Emirates Towers ♿ Excellent

MEYDAN COMPLEX
meydan.ae
dubairacingclub.com

Race night at the stylish Meydan racecourse is an important social event in Dubai, and also an opportunity to see some of the finest Arabian horses in action. The track features a 2,624yd (2,400m) long turf course inside a 1,913yd (1,750m) all-weather course, running past the grandstand, with its distinctive crescent-shaped roof. The illegality of gambling in the United Arab Emirates has been circumvented by the giving away of prizes for correct predictions of race results. The whole of Dubai society turns up for the World Cup races in March so if you're lucky enough to get a seat it makes for great people-watching too.

🔼 Off map at B9 ✉ Off Al Ain–Dubai road; signposted from Interchange 1 and 2 of Sheikh Zayed Road ☎ 332 2277 🕐 Race nights: Oct–Apr Thu 7pm ♿ Excellent 🎟 General admission and parking free (except for Dubai World Cup race)

MUSEUM OF THE FUTURE
museumofthefuture.ae

With a remit to become "the world's largest and most exciting home to tomorrow's trends and opportunities" Sheikh Mohammed bin Rashid Al Maktoum wants this museum to be "an incubator for ideas, a driver for innovation, and a destination for inventors and entrepreneurs." With a motto of "See the future, create the future" the building really lives up to the dream, with a unique design by Killa Designs. This is said to be one of the most complex structures in the world, a silver egg shape made up of 890 steel and

Meydan racecourse

Horses and jockeys on the Meydan race track

fiberglass panels with a void (said to represent the future to be explored) swathed in black Arabic script.

🔲 D5 ✉ Sheikh Zayed Road ☎ 440 8888 🕐 Opening in 2019 🚇 Dubai Mall

OLD TOWN

In the heart of high-rise Downtown Dubai (▷ 70) this tiny enclave is a low-rise homage to the traditional Arabic architecture found in old Al Bastakiya (▷ 24) and Shindagha (▷ 32–33) in Bur Dubai. Its alleyways and squares are sprinkled with cafés, and the traditionally styled Souk Al Bahar sells a range of local arts and handicrafts. It's a great place to explore while waiting for the next performance of The Dubai Fountain (▷ 65).

🔲 A6 ✉ Off Sheikh Mohammed bin Rashid Boulevard ☎ Customer Center: 367 3333 🚇 Burj Khalifa/Dubai Mall ♿ Excellent

RAS AL KHOR

Known as the "Cape of the Creek," this is a rare and precious wetland at the head of the 8.5-mile (14km) long Dubai Creek. This tiny sanctuary, only 2.4 sq miles (6.2 sq km) in area, is vital for the 20,000 birds that spend their winters here. The maximum depth of the water is 6.5ft (2m) with a tidal range of between 3.2ft (1m) and 4.9ft (1.5m). It's an environment that supports more than 500 species of flora and fauna—at the peak of the winter season, 67 different species settle here, including dunlins, godwits, curlews, redshanks, little stints and sandwich terns, plus a resident population of flamingos. There are scientifically important numbers of broad-billed sandpipers, and Pacific golden, gray and Kentish plovers. Ospreys hunt and large numbers of black-headed gulls patrol along the creek.

🔲 Off map at D9 ✉ Off Ras Al Khor Road. Three hides: Gurm/Mangrove off Ras Al Khor Road; Fantir/Flamingo at the junction of Al Wasl and Oud Metha Road, and Al Buhaira/Lagoon close to Al Jadef ☎ 606 6822 🕐 Sat–Thu 9–4 ♿ None 🎟 Free

Flamingoes feeding at Ras Al Khor

Shopping

NORTH SHEIKH ZAYED ROAD AND ZABEEL MALLS

This area is home to the big one, The Dubai Mall (▷ 68–69, thedubaimall.com), but there are other quality shopping districts if you'd prefer something smaller and more personal. Souk Al Bahar (soukalbahar.ae) in Downtown Dubai offers excellent choice in handicrafts. In the south of the district, the Gold and Diamond Park (goldanddiamondpark.com) is the modern air-conditioned equivalent of the Gold Souk in Deira—though it lacks the atmosphere. Nearby Al Quoz (▷ 70; alserkalavenue.ae) has a good range of art galleries with reasonably priced one-of-a-kind souvenirs, and more expensive pieces by international artists.

ABDUL SAMAD AL QURASHI

thedubaimall.com

Selling a range of traditional *ittars*, oudh and incenses, this is an excellent location to research some of the rich scents that make up an Arabian fragrance.

➕ B6 ✉ The Dubai Mall ☎ 388 2780 🕐 Sun–Wed 10am–midnight, Thu–Sat 10am–1am 🚇 Burj Khalifa/Dubai Mall

AL SHAREIF GALLERY

pch.ae

This gallery sells handicrafts imported from around the Gulf, including ceramics, inlaid wooden boxes and gilded metalware.

➕ B6 ✉ The Souk, The Dubai Mall ☎ 330 9088 🕐 Sun–Wed 10am–midnight, Thu–Sat 10am–1am 🚇 Burj Khalifa/Dubai Mall

THE AQUARIUM STORE

thedubaimall.com

Although this is the gift shop of the aquarium you don't need to buy a ticket to shop here. There's something for every budget, from keyrings to one-of-a-kind artworks.

➕ B6 ✉ The Dubai Mall ☎ 448 5201 🕐 Sun–Wed 10am–midnight, Thu–Sat 10am–1am 🚇 Burj Khalifa/Dubai Mall

THE CAMEL COMPANY

camelcompany.ae

Everyone loves a camel, so why not stock up on camel-related souvenirs? Mugs, T-shirts and ceramics match cuddly camels of every size.

➕ A6 ✉ Souk Al Bahar, Old Town ☎ 421 0087 🕐 Sat–Thu 10–10, Fri 2–10 🚇 Burj Khalifa/Dubai Mall

CEYLON MASTER GEMS

ceylonmastergems.com

This small jewelers specializes in high-quality colored stones. Come here for sapphires, rubies and emeralds, loose or set in finished pieces.

➕ e1 ✉ Gold and Diamond Park, Interchange 4, Sheikh Zayed Road, Al Quoz (3) ☎ 340 4310 🕐 Sat–Thu 10–10, Fri 4–10

CHETAN

goldanddiamondpark.com

Chetan has an excellent range of diamond and gem jewelry, with many sets of diamond earrings and necklaces.

➕ e1 ✉ Gold and Diamond Park, Interchange 4, Sheikh Zayed Road, Al Quoz (3) ☎ 340 4644 🕐 Sat–Thu 10–10, Fri 4–10

THE COBBLER

thecobbler.ae

An old-fashioned gentleman's emporium selling bespoke leather shoes, and providing high-quality accessories including socks, polishes and brushes. Another branch can be found in The Dubai Mall.

➕ D5 ✉ Dubai International Financial Center ☎ 386 3490 🕐 Sun–Thu 9–7, Sat 9–6. Closed Fri 🚇 Financial Center

CUADRO

caudroart.com

A fine art gallery for the discerning collector with pieces in all genres, plus helpful and knowledgeable staff.

➕ D5 ✉ Gate Village, Dubai International Financial Center ☎ 425 0400 🕐 Sun–Thu 10–8, Sat noon–6 🚇 Financial Center

DAMAS

damasjewellery.com

Internationally renowned jewelers with outlets in 18 countries, Damas stocks ranges by the finest manufacturers including Tiffany & Co and Gucci.

➕ B6 ✉ The Dubai Mall ☎ 339 8846 🕐 Sun–Wed 10am–midnight, Thu–Sat 10am–1am 🚇 Burj Khalifa/Dubai Mall

THE EMPTY QUARTER FINE ART PHOTOGRAPHY

theemptyquarter.com

Currently the only gallery in Dubai dealing exclusively in photographic images, with an impressive collection from around the world, but the local images may be the more appealing.

➕ D5 ✉ Gate Village, Dubai International Financial Center ☎ 323 1210 🕐 Sat–Thu 10–8. Closed Fri 🚇 Financial Center

GALLERY ONE

g-1.com

The best place for affordable prints and art relating to Dubai—these may not be one-of-a-kind, but they certainly have some evocative images.

➕ A6 ✉ Souk Al Bahar, Old Town ☎ 420 3619 🕐 Sat–Thu 10–10, Fri 2–10 🚇 Burj Khalifa/Dubai Mall

HERITAGE CARPET

Heritage Carpet is said to stock the world's largest collection of Persian carpets, this store has examples of everyday rugs to stunning luxury investment pieces.

➕ B6 ✉ Dubai Mall ☎ 221 7271 🕐 Sun–Wed 10am–midnight, Thu–Sat 10am–1am 🚇 Burj Khalifa/Dubai Mall

MOMENTUM

momentum-dubai.com

Momentum stocks an impressive collection of vintage and antique time-pieces, including very rare specimens.

➕ D5 ✉ Dubai International Financial Center ☎ 327 4320 🕐 Sun–Thu 10–8, Sat noon–6. Closed Fri 🚇 Financial Center

MOZAIIC ART GALLERY

This gallery has a well-chosen range of art and ceramics around Arabian and Islamic themes including prints and posters, plus some calligraphy.

➕ A6 ✉ Souk Al Bahar, Old Town ☎ 277 6122 🕐 Sat–Thu 10–10, Fri 2–10

SHOWCASE

showcaseuae.com

With a wide range of Arabia-based artists and representation of many other upcoming artists from around the globe, this gallery offers the chance to buy a unique souvenir of your trip.

➕ Off map at A5 ✉ Unit 35, Akserkel Avenue, Al Quoz ☎ 379 0940 🕐 Sat–Thu 10am–7pm

LITTLE GEMS

When buying gemstones, the price depends on four factors:

● Cut: Is it a good shape? Does it reflect light well?

● Clarity: Are there any inclusions (foreign bodies) in the stone and, if so, how big?

● Color: All gemstones have an ideal color.

● Carat weight: Stones are weighed in carats (each carat is 0.2 grams). Generally, the more a stone weighs the bigger it is.

Entertainment and Nightlife

40 KONG

40kong.com

This open terrace bar on the 40th floor offers panoramic views of the Sheikh Zayed Road skyline. It's a popular meeting spot and late-night hangout with a great wine, spirits and cocktail list and a short menu of food.

F5 ⊠ H Hotel, 1 Sheikh Zayed Road ☎ 355 8896 Daily 7pm–3am World Trade Center

ARMANI/PRIVÉ

armanihotels.com

One of Dubai's coolest clubs in the ultra-chic Armani Hotel in Burj Khalifa, Privé plays to a refined clientele so make sure you dress accordingly.

B6 ⊠ Armani Hotel, Burj Khalifa ☎ 888 3308 Mon–Sat 10pm–3am Burj Khalifa/Dubai Mall

AT.MOSPHERE

atmosphereburjkhalifa.com

The views from this stylish bar 122 floors up in Burj Khalifa are difficult to beat. Obviously you pay a premium for the location, and drinks are more expensive if you choose to sit near the full-length windows. There's also a restaurant. Reservations are required.

B6 ⊠ Burj Khalifa ☎ 888 3828 11.30am–2am Burj Khalifa

BLUE BAR

novotel.com

This long-standing Dubai venue has live jazz and blues on weekends and a recorded repertoire on weekdays. It's a rare chance to get a genuine blues vibe in the city. Food is also available.

E5 ⊠ Novotel, Zabeel Road 2, off Sheikh Zayed Road, Trade Center (1) ☎ 332 0000 Sat–Wed noon–2am, Thu–Fri noon–3am World Trade Center

CIRQUE LE SOIR

cirquelesoirdubai.com

An undeniably unique experience, this nightclub labels itself the "extreme circus" concept. Costume dress is encouraged but if not, dress to impress to make it through the door.

E5 ⊠ The Fairmont Hotel, Sheikh Zayed Road ☎ 050 995 5400 Mon, Wed, Thu 11pm–3am World Trade Center

THE EMIRATES A380 EXPERIENCE

emiratesa380experience.com

This flight simulator allows you to get behind the controls of an Emirates Airlines A380. You can choose one of 12 locations to make your landing.

B6 ⊠ The Dubai Mall ☎ 388 2915 Wed–Sun 10–10, Thu–Sat 10am–midnight Burj Khalifa/Dubai Mall

FEET LOUNGE

feetlounge.ae

Offering Thai massage and reflexology sessions, this small spa makes a great place to restore your energy levels.

Off map ⊠ Executive Towers, Bay Avenue, Business Bay ☎ 452 2259 Sun–Thu noon–10, Fri–Sat 10–10 Business Bay

THE FRIDGE

thefridgedubai.com

One of the leading arts organizations in Dubai, The Fridge supports concerts and exhibitions both at its HQ in Al Quoz and at venues around the city.

Off map ⊠ Off Alserkal Avenue, Al Quoz (1) ☎ 347 7793 Varied calendar

THE GALLERY AT EMAAR PAVILION

emaargallery.com

Dubai property giants Emaar have funded Dubai's most exciting new art

space in the heart of their Downtown Dubai development. The gallery features a program of exhibitions by established and emerging artists.

⊞ A6 ⊠ Mohammed bin Rashid Boulevard, Downtown Dubai ☎ 428 7938 ◉ Sat–Thu 9–6 🚇 Burj Khalifa/Dubai Mall

HYSTERIA HAUNTED ATTRACTION

hysteria.ae

This thoroughly contemporary attraction has more than a hint of the old haunted house fairground attractions, though the special effects take the suspense and gory detail to a whole new level. It's not for the faint hearted and not recommended for young children.

⊞ B6 ⊠ Dubai Mall ☎ 330 8424 ◉ Sat–Wed 10am–midnight, Thu–Sat 10am–1am 🚇 Burj Khalifa/ Dubai Mall

IKANDY

shangri-la.com

The Shangri-La pool deck is transformed as the sun goes down into one of the city's coolest clubs. The clientele is uber-fashionable and the views amazing.

⊞ C5 ⊠ Shangri-La, Sheikh Zayed Road ☎ 405 2703 ◉ Daily 6pm–2am 🚇 Financial Center

KIDZANIA

kidzania.ae

When kids want to play adult for the day, bring them to KidZania. This super-vised role-play attraction allows them to choose from 80 activities, including fire fighter, doctor or TV presenter, and the realistic stage sets mean they get to operate in the KidZania real world.

⊞ B6 ⊠ The Dubai Mall ☎ 800 38224 6255 ◉ Sun–Thu 10–10, Fri–Sat 10am–11pm (ticket office closed 1 hour before) 🚇 Burj Khalifa/Dubai Mall

LEVEL 43 SKY LOUNGE

level43lounge.com

Open throughout the day, this rooftop lounge on the 43rd floor really comes to life in the evenings when the lights of Sheikh Zayed Road and Burj Khalifa look spectacular.

⊞ D5 ⊠ Four Points by Sheraton Sheikh Zayed Road, Trade Center (1) ☎ 323 0343 ◉ Daily 2pm–2am 🚇 Financial Center

REEL CINEMAS

reelcinemas.ae

This is the flagship complex of Reel Cinemas. There are MX4D Motion EFX theaters, and there are extra-comforta-ble leather lounge seats with butler service in the Platinum Movie Suites.

⊞ B6 ⊠ The Dubai Mall ☎ 449 1988 ◉ Showings noon–midnight 🚇 Burj Khalifa/Dubai Mall

THE STABLES

At the Stables you'll experience a lively sports bar with English menu and live soccer on the one hand, and bucking bronco and live bands in the Rodeo Drive section on the other. It attracts a down-to-earth crowd.

⊞ E5 ⊠ Next to the Radisson Royal Hotel, Sheikh Zayed Road, Trade Center (1) ☎ 05 2814 1127 ◉ Daily 6pm–2am 🚇 Trade Center

MOVIES

It takes a while for Hollywood's latest hit movies to filter through to Dubai's cinemas. Every movies has to be assessed by the emirate's film censors, who take a hardline attitude to any controversial themes or sub-ject matter—typically this includes political or sexual content. Movies that are released in Dubai may also be edited for language and other content.

THE THIRD EYE

thirdeyeonline.com

A mind and body center which brings together practitioners from many wellbeing and New Age therapies. Visit here for Reiki energy sessions, chakra awakening and angel readings.

➕ C5 ✉ 1101 Saeed Tower, Sheikh Zayed Road, Trade Center (2) ☎ 055 809 8595 🕐 Calendar of sessions throughout the week 🚇 Emirates Towers

WHITE

whitedubai.com

This massive open-air nightclub is one of the most popular venues in the emirate. There's regular appearances by A-list DJs and performers to add to the usual club mix. The experience is "big" in so many ways, with thousands of people enjoying the energy.

➕ Off map at B9 ✉ Meydan Racecourse ☎ 50 433 0933 🕐 End Sep–late Jun

ZINC

ihg.com

Zinc is a popular nightclub aimed at people who want to party rather than strike a pose. The music is determinedly mainstream and "happy hour" drinks deals are generous.

➕ D–E5 ✉ Crowne Plaza Hotel, Sheikh Zayed Road ☎ 050 199 9271 🕐 Daily 7pm–3am 🚇 Emirates Towers

Where to Eat

ABDEL WAHAB ($$–$$$)

soukalbahar.ae

The contemporary decor is at odds with the traditional Lebanese menu but grab a table on the terrace for great views.

➕ A6 ✉ Souk Al Bahar, Old Town ☎ 423 0988 🕐 Lunch, dinner 🚇 Burj Khalifa/ Dubai Mall

AL MANDALOUN ($–$$)

al-mandaloun.com

For a taste of delicious Lebanese food, try this superb contemporary restaurant.

The cooking covers all bases, including *fattoush*, kebabs and stuffed vine leaves, plus a few surprises.

➕ D5 ✉ Dubai International Financial Center ☎ 363 7474 🕐 Breakfast, lunch, dinner. Closed Sun 🚇 Financial Center

AMAL ($$$)

armanihotels.com

This upscale Indian restaurant is currently one of the go-to places in the emirate. The dishes are exquisitely spiced, the interior "cool" and the views stunning.

➕ B6 ✉ Armani Hotel, Burj Khalifa ☎ 888 3666 🕐 Dinner 🚇 Burj Khalifa/Dubai Mall

CAFÉ HABANA ($$)

cafehabana.com

Great cocktails and Mexican/Latin food in a bar styled like a slice of

Hemingway's Havana, great for a more casual night out.

 A6 ✉ Souk Al Bahar, Old Town ☎ 422 2620 🕐 Dinner 🚇 Burj Khalifa/Dubai Mall

CARLUCCIO'S ($–$$)

carluccios.com

Inspired by Antonio Carluccio's cookery, Carluccio's brings relaxed Italian staples to Dubai, with a range of pizzas, pastas and excellent antipasti. This is celebrity chef dining without the ritzy price tag.

 B6 ✉ The Dubai Mall ☎ 434 1320 🕐 Breakfast, lunch, dinner 🚇 Burj Khalifa/ Dubai Mall

CLAW BBQ ($$)

clawbbq.com

Claw supplies comfort food, southern style, in the heart of Downtown Dubai. Expect starters like peel-n-eat shrimp with buckets of crab claws to follow. Bibs are supplied, just like back in Louisiana.

 A6 ✉ Souk Al Bahar, Old Town ☎ 423 2300 🕐 Lunch, dinner 🚇 Burj Khalifa/ Dubai Mall

EWAAN ($$–$$$)

addresshotels.com

On the waterside at Downtown Dubai, this upscale all-day eatery serves delicious breakfast, lunch and dinner à la carte and buffet menus with European and Middle Eastern dishes. There's also an impressive Friday brunch.

 A6 ✉ Palace Downtown Hotel, Downtown Dubai ☎ 888 3444 🕐 Breakfast, lunch, dinner 🚇 Burj Khalifa/Dubai Mall

EXCHANGE GRILL ($$$)

fairmont.com

The Exchange Grill's dining room can seem austere by Dubai standards but superb steaks and an outstanding wine list create a warm glow. Meat lovers can't help but be satisfied.

 E5 ✉ Fairmont Hotel, Sheikh Zayed Road ☎ 311 8316 🕐 Dinner 🚇 World Trade Center

LA FARINE CAFÉ AND BAKERY ($–$$)

marriott.com

Open 24 hours a day for coffee and pastries, La Farine is great to visit after a night on the town. It also offers one of the best afternoon teas in Dubai.

 Off map ✉ JW Marriott Marquis, Business Bay ☎ 414 3000 🕐 Breakfast, lunch, dinner (24 hours) 🚇 Business Bay

HOI AN ($$$)

shangri-la.com

In a convincing mock-Saigon-style dining room, silk-clad waitresses serve delicious Vietnamese dishes. Starters include Saigon street-vendor soup, a clear broth with translucent noodles, chicken and black mushrooms. For the main course, clay-pot chicken is a tasty, tangy choice.

 C5 ✉ Shangri-La, Sheikh Zayed Road ☎ 405 2703 🕐 Dinner nightly, lunch Fri–Sat 🚇 Financial Center

KARMA KAFÉ ($$)

karma-kafe.com

This cool restaurant, bar and lounge has been a big hit for its Asian menu—inspired by Japan, China and Thailand among others. Come for dinner and stay late for drinks.

 A6 ✉ Souk Al Bahar, Old Town ☎ 423 0909 🕐 Dinner nightly, lunch Fri–Sat 🚇 Burj Khalifa/Dubai Mall

KATANA ($$$)

katana-dubai.com

A large contemporary Japanese restaurant offering a comprehensive

menu. Drop in for sushi and sit up at the bar or take a table in the main seating area to enjoy tempura or meat from the robata grill. There are views across the fountain lake to Burj Khalifa.

➕ A6 ✉ The Address Downtown, Downtown Dubai ☎ 427 8808 ◷ Dinner 🚇 Burj Khalifa/Dubai Mall

MARKETTE ($–$$)

This is French-café-meets-American-fast-food-joint and it's a great place to eat at any time of day. Try the crêpes, which are served with a choice of sweet or savory fillings—they're perfect for a quick refuel while shopping. The breakfast menu is international, with a particularly flavorsome *shakshuka*.

➕ B6 ✉ The Dubai mall ☎ 339 8173 ◷ Breakfast, lunch, dinner 🚇 Burj Khalifa/Dubai Mall

MORELLI'S GELATO ($)

morellisgelato.com

With a menu packed full of ice cream and sundaes it might be difficult to make a choice, but whatever you decide, Morelli's expertise will make it delicious. They've been in business since 1907, so they know ice cream (and know a good hot chocolate too).

➕ B6 ✉ The Dubai Mall ☎ 339 9053 ◷ Lunch, dinner 🚇 Burj Khalifa/Dubai Mall

THE NOODLE HOUSE ($)

thenoodlehouse.com

Several outlets of this chain exist around Dubai. They serve up a choice of tasty and inexpensive noodle and rice dishes, plus other pan-Asian standbys. A good option for a quick, low-cost lunch or dinner.

➕ D5 ✉ The Boulevard, Jumeirah Emirates Towers ☎ 319 8088 ◷ Lunch, dinner 🚇 Emirates Towers

THE RIB ROOM ($$–$$$)

jumeirah.com

Rib Room serves top-flight meat to appreciative and loyal clients. The minimalist decor allows you to concentrate on the food. The Saturday brunch features live jazz music.

➕ D5 ✉ Jumeirah Emirates Towers ☎ 553 0444 ◷ Tue–Sun lunch, dinner 🚇 Financial Center

TAQADO MEXICAN KITCHEN ($)

taqado.com

A tasty, simple mid-shopping option. Choose your meat, filling, toppings plus a side order and there you have it. From burritos to tacos, there are no surprises.

➕ D5 ✉ Gate Building 5, Dubai International Financial Center ☎ 351 5210 ◷ Breakfast, lunch, dinner 🚇 Financial Center

TODD ENGLISH FOOD HALL ($$–$$$)

Celebrity chef Todd English brings his 8-restaurant/12-cuisine "food hall" concept to Dubai. With a wealth of choice inspired by dishes from around the world, open kitchens and all-day dining, this market makes for a great place to eat during your day at the mall or after sightseeing.

➕ B6 ✉ The Dubai Mall ☎ 526 9178 ◷ Breakfast, lunch, dinner 🚇 Burj Khalifa/Dubai Mall

ZAROOB ($–$$)

zaroob.com

If you'd like to try Lebanese cuisine but don't want a budget street café then Zaroob could fit the bill. The decor has an urban-café feel and the menu is right on the button.

➕ D5 ✉ Jumeirah Emirates Towers ☎ 327 6262 ◷ Breakfast, lunch, dinner (24 hours) 🚇 Emirates Towers

Jumeirah and Dubai Marina

Dubai's coastline has been transformed beyond recognition in the last 15 years in ways that push the boundaries of engineering expertise. From the dazzling new Dubai Marina, with its forest of high-rise towers, to the first of Dubai's mega-artificial islands, Palm Jumeirah, it plays host to a plethora of luxury beach resorts.

Top 25

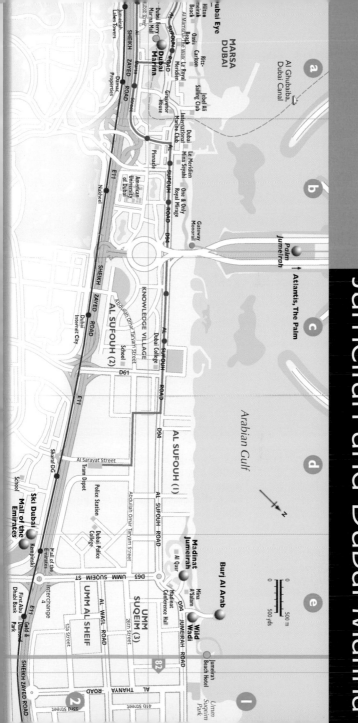

Jumeirah and Dubai Marina

Atlantis, The Palm

TOP 25

TIPS

● Hotel guests get free or reduced entry into some Atlantis attractions.
● Advance purchase will save you money at Dolphin Bay.
● Dolphin Bay tickets include a day-pass to Aquaventure Waterpark.

Dubai's mega-resort is a veritable city within a city. Erupting out of the farthest point of The Palm like a pink wedding cake, the iconic structure is a pleasure dome for vacationers.

The hotel This is the biggest by far in Dubai. It has more than 1,500 rooms, with over 20 eateries and several bars, lounges and nightclubs, all set on 0.8 miles (1.4km) of golden beach.

Aquaventure Waterpark There's excitement here for every age group. The Tower of Neptune area features a nine-story-high slide, and a tube slide through shark-infested waters. The Tower of Poseidon area, meanwhile, plays host to one of the world's largest waterslides and the UAE's first dual-racing loop ride. Kids

Families can enjoy action-packed waterslides and close encounters with sea creatures when visiting Atlantis

have their own specially designed area, Splashers, or they can make sandcastles on Aquaventure Waterpark's private beach.

Dolphin Bay Several different "interactive" experiences are on offer, either in shallow or deeper water. The Dolphin Encounter is perfect for non-swimmers, while the Royal Swim is the ultimate package. At Sea Lion Point you can also take part in Sea Lion Discovery interactive sessions, or drop by for a "kiss 'n' cuddle" snap.

The Lost Chambers Aquarium Enter into a world inspired by the myth of the lost under-water city of Atlantis, where the ruins of old mansions and palaces house 20 tanks of differ-ent marine environments, home to more than 65,000 fish and marine creatures.

THE BASICS

atlantisthepalm.com
🔆 Off map at c1
✉ Crescent Road, The Palm
☎ Hotel reservations
426 2000
🕐 Open daily.
Aquaventure Waterpark:
daily 10am–sunset; The
Lost Chambers Aquarium:
daily 10am–midnight;
Dolphin Bay and Sea lion
Point: daily—sessions must
be reserved in advance.
🚉 Palm monorail
♿ Very good
🖐 Activities expensive

Burj Al Arab

TOP 25

Skyview Bar at Burj Al Arab (left); the exterior of Burj Al Arab is city landmark

THE BASICS

burj-al-arab.com

➕ e1

✉ Beach Road, Jumeirah

☎ 301 7777

♿ Excellent

💵 Expensive (minimum spend per person at the bar)

🏨 Jumeirah Beach Hotel

DID YOU KNOW?

The helipad atop the Burj Al Arab has been the venue of various sporting PR opportunities. In 2004, Tiger Woods teed off; in 2005, Roger Federer and Andre Agassi served and volleyed; in 2011 Rory McIlroy chipped out of a specially prepared bunker for a hole-in-one; and in 2013, David Coulthard burned rubber with some power donuts F1-style in a Red Bull speed machine.

One of the world's most recognizable contemporary buildings, Burj Al Arab broke the mold and—as the world's first seven-star hotel—redefined the luxury hospitality business. It also launched Dubai as a first-class tourist destination.

Inspiration It's fitting that Dubai's iconic building isn't a government edifice, a historic landmark or a place of worship. Architect Thomas Wills Wright was briefed to create something that would signal Dubai's ambitions to the world, but there are also references to Dubai's seafaring past in the sail-like facade made of a Teflon-coated, woven glass-fiber material. Inside it's a riot of color and, if it looks like gold, it probably is: 17,000sq ft (1,600sq m) of gold leaf was used. The hotel's other vital statistics are equally jaw-dropping: there are 1,500 members of staff for 202 suites, each of which has its own butler. A fleet of white Rolls-Royces is at the disposal of guests, while a helicopter shuttle service from the airport costs 10,500 AED per single person, 12,075 per couple.

Visiting The Burj Al Arab stands on its own man-made island 918ft (280m) offshore; if you're not staying here you'll need a reservation at one of the hotel's restaurants or bars to get inside. Admire the view along the coast from the high-level bar over a cocktail. Just as satisfying is to admire its elegance from the outside, especially during the evening light show.

Dubai Eye

The Dubai Eye (Ain Dubai) is the biggest Ferris Wheel in the world. Its gently rounded outline can be seen from around the south of the emirate and the 360-degree views from this rotating platform are spectacular.

The Dubai Eye experience At 689ft (210m) high, Dubai Eye takes 48 minutes to make one full rotation and you can see landmarks such as the Burj Al Arab and Burj Khalifa. There are 48 passenger capsules with 323sq ft (30sq m) of floor space. These can accommodate around 40 people and are spacious enough to allow you to walk around to make the most of the views. Six capsules have refreshments facilities including a bar, and capsules can also be converted into dining pods which can be privately hired for that spectacular meal with a view. If you are daring enough, there's a rope climbing platform on one of the legs where you can enjoy the experience with a qualified instructor.

Bluewaters Island Dubai Eye is set on Bluewaters Island, a small man-made offshore development, linked to the mainland by a pedestrian bridge and separate road. Dubai Eye is part of a large entertainment and retail hub with 200 shops and restaurants and a planned Madame Tussaud's attraction. There are high-quality low-rise residential developments and two luxury hotels with private beaches, with an automated rapid transport system getting you around the island.

THE BASICS

bluewatersdubai.ae
- Off map at a1
- Bluewaters Island
- Check online
- Check online for details
- Nakheel Harbours and Towers
- Automated rapid transport system
- Excellent
- Expensive

DID YOU KNOW?

- The Eye stands 689ft (210m) tall.
- The outer rim weighs 7500 tons.
- 192 cables link the hub with the rim.
- Each cable can take the force of 300 tons.
- A maximum of 1,400 people can ride at any one time.

HIGHLIGHTS

- The impressive dimensions
- The magnificent views

Jumeirah Mosque

DID YOU KNOW?

If you miss seeing Jumeirah Mosque on your trip, you'll find an image of it on the 500 AED bank note.

DRESS CODE

Male and female visitors are expected to dress conservatively, covering arms and legs, and women should also wear a headscarf.

Jumeirah Mosque is the largest and most graceful mosque in the city, and it's the only one in Dubai regularly open to non-Muslims, offering visitors the chance to explore Islamic faith and architecture.

The architecture The mosque was built in 1975 in the medieval Fatimid style—the first flowering of Islamic architecture during the 9th–11th centuries—and is inspired by a larger mosque in Cairo, Egypt. The facade of the mosque has filigree stonework intended to add depth and warmth to the exterior. Inside, the deliberately low-key decoration has Turkish and Egyptian influences. A square arrangement of pillars supports the *qubba*, a central, painted dome, while the imam, or leader, faces Mecca from the *mehrab*, his pulpit.

The elegant Jumeirah Mosque, with its domed roofs and two minarets, is stunning both inside and out

Etiquette for worshipers Shoes are removed before entering the mosque as a sign of respect for other worshipers as Muslims pray and prostrate themselves on the floor. There is no physical distance between worshipers because everyone is equal: the sheikh prays alongside the taxi driver. A separate wing, behind the wooden doors to the left, is the women's prayer section—women don't worship with men in the United Arab Emirates. The hour-long morning tour with a guide from the Sheikh Mohammed Center for Cultural Understanding (▷ 30) gives you a chance to admire not just the interior of the mosque, but also to find out more about the Muslim faith as questions are encouraged and answered honestly. This is not a platform for proselytizing and the whole encounter is gently informative.

THE BASICS

cultures.ae

✚ E2

✉ Beach Road

☎ 353 6666

🕐 Tours for non-Muslims at 10am (though it's advisable to get there early) on Sat–Thu with a guide from the Sheikh Mohammed Center for Cultural Understanding (▷ 30)

♿ Few

💷 Inexpensive

🏖 Jumeirah Open Beach

Madinat Jumeirah

Arabian chic at Madinat Jumeirah beach resort

TOP 25

THE BASICS

madinatjumeirah.com
🞢 e1
✉ Beach Road, at Umm Suqeim Road
☎ 366 8888
🍴 Many good cafés, restaurants and bars
♿ Good
🚌 Jumeirah Beach Hotel

HIGHLIGHTS

● The range of fashionable restaurants and bars
● The handicrafts in the stylized souk
● *Abra* rides along the canals

Madinat Jumeirah was Dubai's first planned tourism complex. A theme-park-style homage to Arabic architecture that some may find kitsch—think *One Thousand and One Nights*—it buzzes with energy.

What's here With three boutique hotels, 40 restaurants, a handful of entertainment venues and a shopping mall, Madinat Jumeirah is a self-contained resort. Among the towering *barjeels*, 2.5 miles (4km) of waterways, complete with motorized *abras* (extra cost) and a specially created shipwreck, snake around the property, and lush greenery completes the oasis effect.

Souk Madinat It's air-conditioned and the prices are fixed, but this is a film-set fantasy of what a genuine souk could have looked like. With only 70 shops, it is compact when compared to others in Dubai. There's a leaning toward quality regional crafts here, so the shops have more carpets, Arabic antiques and arts than fashion labels—in keeping with the theme.

After dark Madinat Theatre is an intimate 442-seat space with a varied program. Outside, live-music events are staged in the 4,500-seater amphitheater Madinat Arena, which has an atmospheric setting surrounded by canals, palm trees and traditional *barjeels*. Many of Madinat Jumeirah's restaurants have a canal-side setting which makes them perfect for a cozy or romantic dinner.

You can ski (left and right) or toboggan (center) among other attractions at Ski Dubai

TOP 25

Ski Dubai

Snow skiing in the desert—an impossible dream or the height of folly one might think, but not in Dubai. The 25-story-high Ski Dubai indoor ski slope is one of the city's most remarkable attractions.

Indoor marvel Even by looking into Ski Dubai from the viewers' gallery at the Mall of the Emirates (▷ 93), you can see what a technological achievement the construction is. Quad chairlifts relay skiers up to the top of 242,187sq ft (22,500sq m) of piste, which includes, including the world's first indoor black run. Runs are up to 278ft (85m) high, 262ft (80m) wide and 1,312ft (400m) long, so there's enough space for 1,500 skiers and boarders at any one time. Everywhere is frosted with snow, created by what is, in simple terms, a giant air-conditioning system. Up to 30 tons of snow is made daily. Insulation keeps Ski Dubai cool even in the summer months—the designers describe it as the world's largest refrigerator.

Fun on the snow If you're not cut out for skiing, there's always Snowpark, where you can explore a snow cavern or take a trip down the toboggan run. The Snow Bullet is the first sub-zero zipline ride in the world.

Snow penguins Ski Dubai also has some rather different permanent residents: a group of gentoo and king penguins who "march" through the snow every 2 hours from 2pm until 8pm. You can also arrange penguin encounters.

THE BASICS

theplaymania.com/skidubai

🞦 d2

✉ Mall of the Emirates, Interchange 4, Sheikh Zayed Road

☎ 800 386

🕐 Sat–Tue 10am–11pm (last ticket 9.30), Wed–Fri 10am–midnight

🚇 Mall of the Emirates

♿ Good Avalanche Café ($–$$)

✋ Expensive

HIGHLIGHTS

- The Alpine atmosphere
- The black run
- The snowball arena
- The cute penguin march

TIPS

- Ski Dubai is very popular, so reserve ahead on weekends.
- It provides all equipment except gloves.
- You'll need to show certain skill levels on the slopes—or take lessons.

JUMEIRAH AND DUBAI MARINA TOP 25

More to See

DUBAI MARINA
The centerpiece of a second axis to the city, Dubai Marina combines leisure and residential facilities on a waterway that runs inland around the hotels of Al Sufouh. It's a man-made harbor surrounded by 100 skyscrapers and a 4.3-mile (7km) walkway. By the sea, Jumeirah Beach Residence is a complex of five high-rise towers linked by The Walk, a boulevard with 300 shopping and dining outlets. XLine (xdubai.com), the world's longest urban zipline, runs from 557ft (170m) up across the marina.
➕ a1 ✉ Off Sheikh Zayed Road, west of Al Sufouh ☎ 362 7900 🚇 Damac
🚋 Tram: Jumeirah Beach Residence 1 & 2, Dubai Marina Mall, Dubai Marina ♿ Good
🚢 Dubai Ferry Marina Mall

IRANIAN MOSQUE
The most incredible mosque in Dubai, the Imam Hussein Mosque (known as the Iranian Mosque) is also one of the smallest. The diminutive mosque, set on a crossroads a couple of blocks from Jumeirah Mosque (▷ 88–89), has a distinctive onion-shaped dome influenced by the Persian architectural style and blanketed in thousands of colored tiles.
➕ E3 ✉ Off 2A Street, Jumeirah 1
☎ 344 2886 🕐 Not open to non-Muslims
♿ None

JUMEIRAH BEACH PARK
This pay-to-enter beach is definitely worth the small fee. Along with sandy beaches patrolled by life guards, BBQ areas, a 4.3 mile (7km) cycle track and shady gardens, you'll find the outlet of the Dubai Canal, an artificial waterway linking the coast with Dubai Creek. You can take water taxis and pleasure trips inland along the canal, which has new districts developing.
➕ j1 ✉ Beach Road, Jumeirah 2 ☎ 349 2111 🕐 Sun–Wed 8am–10pm, Thu–Sat 8am–11pm. Sun and Wed ladies only
♿ Good 💷 Inexpensive. Additional fee for sunbeds and parasols, inexpensive
🚢 Jumeirah Beach Park

The tiled exterior of the Iranian Mosque

LA MER

lamerdubai.ae

With its wooden boardwalk, driftwood beach huts and grassy verges, La Mer has a surf-resort feel that makes it definitely the most relaxed beach complex along Dubai's coast. Designed to be eco-friendly, it's low rise and colorful too—but still offers visitors 130 shops and a host of places to eat. Alongside the long, sandy beach the main attraction is Laguna Water Park (lagunawaterpark.com), with the WaveOz 180 FloRider, and other rides and relaxing pools.

🔹 D2 ✉ Jumeirah Beach Road ☎ 800 637 227 🕐 Sun–Wed 10–10, Thu–Sat 10–midnight 🚤 Water taxi stops at La Mer Marine Transport Station ♿ Excellent 💷 Laguna Water Park expensive, beach hut rental expensive

MAJLIS GHORFAT UM AL SHEEF

Dubai's future was finalized at this modest house. It was here, in the late 1950s, that discussions took place about how the emirate could transfrom. The complex was constructed in 1955 and was used by the late Sheikh Rashid bin Saeed Al Maktoum as a summer resort when the area was populated by fishermen living in beachside *barastis* (straw huts); today, surrounded by suburban villas, it can seem rather underwhelming.

🔹 j1 ✉ Signposted from the corner of Beach Road and 17th Street, by the HSBC bank ☎ 394 6343 🕐 Sat–Thu 9am–midnight, Fri 3.30–8.30 💷 Inexpensive ♿ Few 🏖 Jumeirah Beach Park

MALL OF THE EMIRATES

malloftheemirates.com

Dubai's second major mall (after The Dubai Mall, ▷ 68–69), with over 550 shops and entertainment and activity centers. The biggest outlets are the department stores Debenhams and Harvey Nichols. On the first floor you'll find the Magic Planet children's zone and the supervised Peekaboo play area for younger children, as well as the

Under the Fashion Dome in the Mall of the Emirates

On the beach at Jumeirah

Vox cinema complex and Dubai's second theater venue, the Dubai Community Arts Theatre.

➕ e2 ✉ Interchange 4, Sheikh Zayed Road ☎ 409 9000 🕐 Sun–Wed 10–10, Thu–Sat 10–midnight 🍴 Many restaurants and cafés 🚇 Mall of the Emirates ♿ Good

PALM JUMEIRAH

The first of Dubai's mega offshore land reclamation projects to reach fruition, Palm Jumeirah is the smallest of the three palm islands originally greenlit. It's now a fully functioning community, complete with over 20 luxury hotels, including Atlantis, The Palm (▷ 84–85).

➕ b1 ✉ Off Jumeirah Beach Road 🍴 Many restaurants and cafés 🚇 Palm Monorail ♿ Generally good

UMM SUQEIM BEACH

This public beach offers great views of Burj Al Arab (▷ 86) just offshore. It's also known locally as Kite Beach because it's here that the kite-surfers gather when the onshore winds are blowing. Nearby

Umm Suqeim Park is a low-key place for families to relax, with a play area and cafés on site.

➕ g1 ✉ Jumeirah Beach Road ☎ Park: 348 5665 🕐 Park: Sat–Wed 8am–11pm, Thu–Fri 8am–11.30pm (Sun–Wed women and children only) ♿ Good

WILD WADI

wildwadi.com

Dubai's first water park, 12-acre (5ha) Wild Wadi is still as popular as ever. Try Jumeirah Sceirah (pronounced "scarer") ride, with a 32m (105ft) drop and speeds of 80kph (50mph) or Tantrum Alley, a tube ride through exciting artificial tornadoes. Younger visitors can enjoy the family play area in Juha's Dhow and Lagoon, or ride Juha's Journey lazy river. You can also learn to surf in the specially designed WipeOut and Riptide Flowrider.

➕ e1 ✉ Beach Road ☎ 348 4444 🕐 Nov–Feb daily 10–6; Mar–May and Sep–Oct daily 10–7; Jun–Aug daily 10–8 ♿ Good 💰 Expensive 🚌 Jumeirah Beach Hotel

Palm Jumeirah

Family-fun can be had at Wild Wadi

Shopping

JUMEIRAH AND DUBAI MARINA MALLS

Mall of the Emirates (▷ 93) is the flagship of this area, with Souk Madinat (▷ 90) taking the crown for design. There are excellent ranges of shops at Dubai Marina Mall (dubaimarinamall.com) and The Walk (thewalkdubai.com), both in Dubai Marina. The new low-rise coastal shopping zone at La Mer (▷ 93) is also worth exploring; it's on a smaller scale than the mega malls, with a relaxed village vibe.

AL JABER GALLERY

A one stop-shop for souvenirs of Dubai, from kitsch models of Burj Khalifa, "I Love Dubai" T-shirts, camels and mugs with amusing messages, to Arabian crafts, and also collectibles.
🔛 d2 ⊠ Mall of the Emirates ☎ 341 4103
🕐 Daily 10–10 🚇 Mall of the Emirates

D.TALES

design-tales.com
Selling furniture, soft furnishings, homeware and gift items produced by Scandinavian designers, it offers a contrast to the multicolored traditional Arabian design.
🔛 B2 ⊠ Jumeirah Beach Road, Jumeirah (3)
☎ 338 6395 🕐 Tue–Sat 9.30–8.30, Sun–Mon 9.30–6.30

MAGRUDY'S

magrudy.com
Everybody's favorite bookstore, Magrudy's is where expat kids head for schoolbooks and everyone shops for the latest blockbuster, and it's been this way since 1975. Visitors will love their Dubai coffeetable souvenir editions.
🔛 E2 ⊠ Magrudy Mall, Beach Road, Jumeirah (1) ☎ 297 9191 🕐 Sat–Thu 9am–10pm, Fri 2–10

NATIONAL IRANIAN CARPETS

niccarpets.com
Founded in 1917, this family company has established a reputation for supplying excellent handwoven rugs and carpets in the Persian tradition. The family originated in Esfahan just east of Tehran, and now imports silk and wool carpets and rugs from across Iran.
🔛 e1 ⊠ Souk Madinat, Madinat Jumeirah
☎ 368 6002 🕐 Daily 10am–11.30pm

SHAYMARTIAN

The perfect place to shop for beachwear for the whole family, Sheymartian has elegant styles by a range of international brands, plus accessories such as bags, caps and beach sandals.
🔛 D2 ⊠ La Mer Mall ☎ 50 679 8108
🕐 Sun–Thu 10–10, Fri–Sat 10am–midnight

SNOW PRO

Yes, as the name suggests, it caters to clients of Ski Dubai (▷ 91) and sells a wide range of ski equipment and clothing. Come to the desert to buy your slope gear.
🔛 e2 ⊠ Mall of the Emirates ☎ 409 4141
🕐 Sat–Wed 10am–midnight, Thu–Fri 10am–1am 🚇 Mall of the Emirates

---

MARINA MARKET

In the cooler months, Dubai Marina Mall Promenade holds an excellent outdoor arts and handicrafts market every weekend, with local artists offering handcrafted items, fashion accessories and decorative things for the home, and stalls selling coffee beans, honey and other foodstuffs. It's a wonderful place to browse to see what Dubai's creative community is putting out. See marinamarket.ae.
🕐 Oct–Apr Wed 10–10, Thu–Sat 10am–11pm

Entertainment and Nightlife

101

oneandonlythepalm.com

There are wonderful views across to Dubai Marina from the deck of this lounge bar. Take the boat transfer from the One&Only Royal Mirage for the most dramatic arrival.

b1 One&Only The Palm, Palm Jumeirah 440 1030 Daily 11am–1am

BARASTI BAR

barastibeach.com

This perennial favorite is a beach resort by day but one of the coolest beach bars at night.

b1 Le Meridien Mina Seyahi Beach Resort and Marina, Al Sufouh Road 318 1313 Wed–Sat 11am–1.30am, Thu–Fri 11am–3pm Tram: Mina Seyahi

BASTIEN GONZALEZ PEDI:MANI:CURE

bastiengonzalez.com

This celebrity podiatrist's unique approach to foot-care makes it worth the high price tag. The flawless nail finish lasts for months.

Off map at c1 One&Only The Palm, Palm Jumeirah 440 1040 Daily 10–10 Palm Monorail

DUKITE

dukite.com

Offering lessons for beginners and improvers, Dukite is the leader in instruction of this incredibly popular sport.

f1 Office Fishing Harbor, Umm Suqeim (3), lessons held at Kite Beach 50 758 6992 Daily 10am–9pm

DUSAIL

dusail.com

Dusail has boats of every kind for charter. Enjoy an hour trip along the

coast or rent for longer to really enjoy the creek.

b1 Dubai International Marine Club, Mina Seyahi, Al Sufouh Road 050 551 7280 Tram: Media City

EMIRATES GOLF CLUB

dubaigolf.com

Treading the same greens as the champions is a cinch in Dubai. A new course designed by Sir Nick Faldo now offers more choice.

b2 Off Sheikh Zayed Road Reservations: 380 1234

LITTLE WORLD DISCOVERY CENTRE

littleworlduae.com

A sensory and educational world of fun for children. Split into 15 discovery zones with hands-on activities.

D2 La Mer, Jumeirah Beach Road 349 9689 Sun–Thu 10–10, Fri–Sat 10am–midnight No transport

LOCK, STOCK & BARREL

lsbdubai.com

This huge contemporary sports bar and lounge is the place to meet partying ex-pats with regular live music.

a1 Rixos Premium Dubai, JBR The Walk 392 7120 Mon–Thu 4pm–3am, Fri 1pm–3am, Sat–Sun 2pm–3am Tram :Jumeirah Beach Residence 1

MADINAT THEATRE

madinattheatre.com

A beautifully styled theater with shows from ballet to Sesame Street musicals.

e1 Madinat Jumeirah 366 6546

NASIMI BEACH

atlantisthepalm.com

The spacious terrace overlooks the golden beach at Atlantis. In the

afternoon enjoy the resident DJ's choice of tracks as you sunbathe. After dark, kick off your shoes and dance barefoot in the sand.

⊞ Off map at c1 ⊠ Atlantis, The Palm, Palm Jumeirah ☎ 426 2626 ⏱ Daily 11am–2am 🚊 Palm monorail

PAVILION DIVE CENTER

jumeirah.com

The only PADI 5-star dive center in the UAE, at the Pavilion Diver Center you'll find excellent instruction and the warm waters are perfect for dive training.

⊞ e1 ⊠ Jumeirah Beach Hotel, Jumeirah Road, Umm Suqeim (3) ☎ 406 8828

SKY AND SEA

watersportsdubai.com

You'll find a whole range of water sports at this family-owned company. Take a fun ride on a donut or learn to dive.

⊞ a1 ⊠ Hilton Dubai Jumeirah Resort, Dubai Marina ☎ 399 9005 ⏱ Office open 9–8 for reservations 🚊 Damac 🚊 Tram: Jumeirah Beach Residence 1 & 2

SKYDIVE DUBAI

skydivedubai.ae

With unsurpassed views on the way down, try tandem skydiving to a site on the coast—the ultimate adrenaline rush.

⊞ a1 ⊠ Al Seyahi St, Mina Seyahi, The Palm ☎ 4377 8888 ⏱ By appointment

Where to Eat

PRICES
Prices are approximate, based on a 3-course meal for one person. $$$ over 300 AED $$ 150–300 AED $ under 150 AED

AL FAYROOZ LOUNGE ($$)

jumeirah.com

Filled with Persian carpets, and rattan and leather furniture reminiscent of an Agatha Christie film location, this is a great spot for afternoon tea.

⊞ e1 ⊠ Madinat Jumeirah ☎ 366 6730 ⏱ Breakfast, lunch, afternoon tea and dinner

THE BEACH BAR & GRILL ($$)

oneandonlyresorts.com

With a wooden deck overlooking the shoreline, this is an excellent place for

an al fresco lunch or candlelit dinner. The menu is surf and turf.

⊞ b1 ⊠ One&Only Royal Mirage, Al Sufouh ☎ 399 9999 ⏱ Lunch, dinner 🚊 Tram: Media City or Palm Jumeirah

BICE ($$–$$$)

hilton.com

Bice is one of the best Italian restaurants in the city. Meat and seafood dominate the menu, although you can order a simple, if luxurious, pasta dish if you prefer.

⊞ a1 ⊠ Hilton Dubai Jumeirah Resort, Dubai Marina ☎ 318 2520 ⏱ Lunch, dinner 🚊 Dubai Tram

BUSSOLA ON THE BEACH ($–$$$)

bussoladubai.com

Sea views and a choice of 32 good, value pizzas add to the appeal of this

Italian restaurant, which has an open-air veranda. À la carte can be expensive.
🔳 b1 ✉ Westin Mina Seyahi, Al Sufouh Road, Al Sufouh ☎ 511 7373 🕔 Lunch, dinner. Closed Jun–Sep 🚋 Tram: Mina Seyahi

FUMÉ ($$)
fume-eatery.com
Manhattan loft-style decor and a fusion menu make this one of the most popular eateries in the marina. Arrive early or you'll need to wait in line.
🔳 a1 ✉ Dubai Marina ☎ 421 5669
🕔 Lunch, dinner 🚇 Damac 🚋 Tram: Dubai Marina Mall

HANOI NATURALLY ($)
hanoinaturally.com
An airy contemporary eatery serving inexpensive Vietnamese food. Fragrant soups and crispy salads make great light lunches. The noodle dishes will satisfy a bigger appetite.
🔳 a2 ✉ Gold Crest Building, Jumeirah Lake Towers ☎ 431 3099 🕔 Lunch, dinner
🚇 Jumeirah Lake Towers 🚋 Tram: Jumeirah Lake Towers

INDEGO BY VINEET ($$$)
indegobyvineet.com
Chef Vineet Bhatia's stellar Indian restaurant melds traditional Indian cooking with contemporary techniques, and it's won him a Michelin star. Delicate desserts help cool the spicy main dishes.
🔳 a1 ✉ Grosvenor House, Dubai Marina
☎ 317 6000 🕔 Lunch, dinner 🚋 Tram: Jumeirah Beach Residence 1

NATHAN OUTLAW AT AL MAHARA ($$$)
The 7-star Burj's signature restaurant serves seafood in a marine environment featuring a central column aquarium. The menu, overseen by English chef Nathan Outlaw, is carefully crafted and appropriately expensive.
🔳 e1 ✉ Burj Al Arab ☎ 301 7600
🕔 Lunch, dinner. Children are welcome at lunchtime only

RONDA LOCATELLI ($$$)
atlantisthepalm.com
Celebrity chef Giorgio Locatelli serves up fresh regional Italian dishes at the Atlantis mega-resort. Try Milanese-style *osso bucco* or tagliolini with octopus in a spicy sauce.
🔳 Off map at c1 ✉ Atlantis, The Palm
☎ 426 2626 🕔 Lunch, dinner 🚋 Palm monorail

SPLENDIDO ($$$)
ritzcarlton.com
With a sun-soaked terrace, views over the Gulf and a menu of simple, classic dishes, Splendido has hit a winning and crowd-pleasing formula.
🔳 a1 ✉ Ritz-Carlton, Al Sufouh Road
☎ 399 4000 🕔 Lunch, dinner 🚋 Tram Jumeirah Beach Residence 1

TOROTORO ($$–$$$)
torotoro-dubai.com
Richard Sandoval's fusion ceviche dishes are mouth-watering, and you can eat tapas-style, choosing from a long menu —perfect if you have trouble deciding.
🔳 a1 ✉ Grosvenor House, Dubai Marina
☎ 317 6000 🕔 Dinner 🚋 Tram: Jumeirah Beach Residence 1

ZATAAR W ZEIT ($)
zataarwzeit.net
For a snack, light lunch or late supper enjoy a tasty budget *shwarma* from this small, modern fast-food style café.
🔳 a1 ✉ Marina View Towers, Dubai Marina
☎ 451 3616 🕔 Lunch and dinner 🚇 Damac 🚋 Tram: Marina Mall or Dubai Marina

Farther Afield

Dubai's metropolitan sprawl has plenty to keep urbanites happy but beyond the city limits it's another world. With rolling sand dunes and arid scrubland as far as the eye can see, there's plenty of opportunity for adventure sport and wilderness experiences.

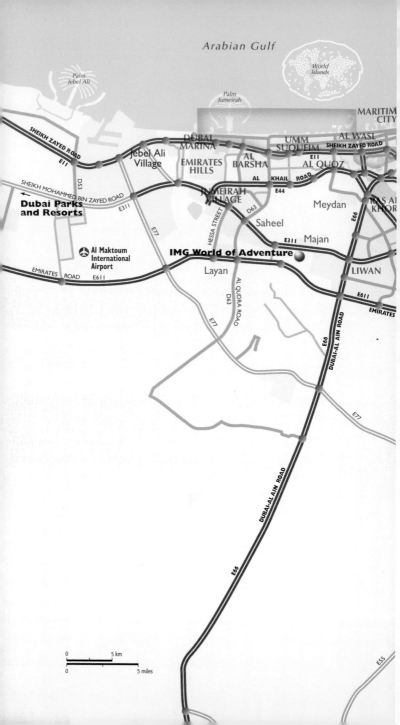

DUBAI

BUR DUBAI

AL MAMZAR

SHARJAH

AJMAN

ZAWRA

HAMRIYA

DEIRA

E11

E11

D79

Dubai International Airport

INDUSTRIAL AREAS

ZAHRA

JURF

E55

BIN ZAYED ROAD

MOHAMMED

E311

E68

E311

D62

SHEIKH

E311

AL MIZHAR

Sharjah International Airport

HELIO

WARSAN

E44

E102

EMIRATES ROAD

ROAD

E611

Al Awir

AL AWIR ROAD

E44

AL DHAID ROAD

E88

Lahbab

E102

SHARJA-KALBA ROAD

Al Dhaid

Dubai Desert Conservation Reserve

MADAM ROAD

E44

Arabian Desert

E55

E55

Al Madam

E102

N

Farther Afield

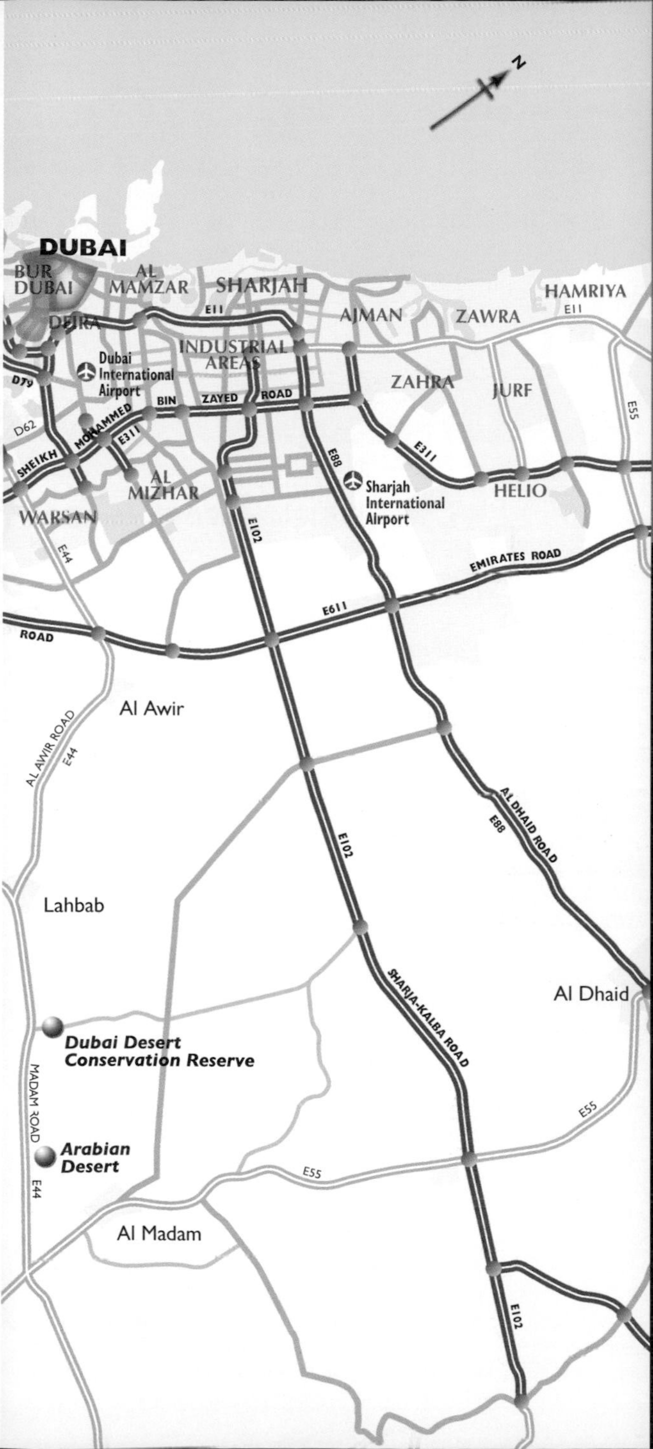

Arabian Desert

You can drive a 4x4 (left) or horse-ride (right) in the Arabian Desert

THE BASICS

☩ Off map
✉ East of the city, off the Hatta road
✋ Activities expensive (▷ 103, 106)

HIGHLIGHTS

● Seemingly never-ending sand dunes
● The star-strewn skies after dark
● Relaxing over a mezze meal in a Bedouin camp
● Breaking the crest on a dune buggy

TIPS

● Take precautions in the heat. Think water, hat and sunscreen.
● If you want to see a selection of nocturnal desert animals, head to Dubai Aquarium & Underwater Zoo (▷ 64)
Safari Companies:
● Arabian Adventures arabian-adventures.com
● Dubai Desert Safari Tours desertsafaritours.com

It's easy to forget that Dubai is a desert city, but a short journey inland and you'll discover a completely different world.

Tip of the iceberg The Arabian Desert is vast, stretching 900,000sq miles (2.3 million sq km) across the Arabian Peninsula. Dubai occupies a transition zone in the northeastern corner, meaning its "desert" is quite varied, with barren rolling dunes sitting cheek by jowl with semi-arid scrubland. The desert supports a complicated ecosystem, though Dubai's largest animal, the Arabian oryx, is critically endangered. Apex predators—desert foxes and two species of cat—are small in stature. They hunt prey including hares, rodents and lizards, though the biggest of these, the desert monitor, might prove too formidable. By day butterflies, dragonflies, locusts and mantises take to the air. As the sun sets, the night shift takes over in the form of several species of bats and moths.

Desert activities Today the desert is a playground for Emiratis and visitors alike. Carefully controlled zones have become racetracks for powerful 4x4s where you can put your foot on the accelerator and let off steam, climb the ridge of a sand wave in a dune buggy or glide down it on a sand-board. You can also spend time as a Bedouin at a desert camp with a desert feast, camel rides and falconry displays. It's a great way to forget about urban life, even for just a little while. Camps offer lunch, dinner, full-day or overnight experiences.

More to See

DUBAI DESERT CONSERVATION RESERVE

ddcr.org

Dubai Desert Conservation Reserve covers 86sq miles (225sq km) of dunes and gravel plains in the southeast of the emirate and is dedicated to conserving the biodiversity of the Arabian Desert, including the desert oryx. But it also offers a chance to experience both traditional and modern Arab pursuits through local tour companies.

➕ Off map ✉ Off Al Ain Road ☎ DDCR: 809 8710; Al Maha Desert Resort & Spa: 832 9900 ⏱ Daily, by organized tour ♿ Few 💷 Expensive

DUBAI PARKS AND RESORTS

Dubaiparksandresorts.com

With four parks and over 100 rides, several entertainment companies have come together to create a mega theme park. Legoland Dubai and Legoland Waterpark are joined by Motiongate Dubai—branded entertainment from DreamWorks Animation, Columbia Pictures and Lionsgate, plus Smurfs Village and Bollywood Parks Dubai.

➕ Off map ✉ Off Sheikh Zayed Road, Jebel Ali ☎ 820 0000 ⏱ Legoland Dubai and Legoland Waterpark open daily but varying hours. Motiongate Apr–mid Sep Sat–Wed 3pm–8pm, Thu–Fri 3pm–9pm; mid Sep–May daily 11–11. Bollywood Dubai Apr–mid Sep daily 3pm–11pm; mid Sep–Mar Wed–Sat 1pm–9pm, Fri–Sat 1pm–11pm 🍴 Numerous eateries 🚌 Free shuttle from major shopping malls and hotels ♿ Very good 💷 Expensive

IMG WORLD OF ADVENTURE

imgworlds.com

This indoor theme park has four adventure zones. Marvel features favorite Marvel comic/film characters including Spider-Man and Ironman, while Lost Valley heads back to the Jurassic era, and you can ride with The Powerpuff Girls at Cartoon Network.

➕ Off map ✉ Off Sheikh Mohammed bin Zayed Road ☎ 403 8888 ⏱ Sun–Wed 11–8, Thu–Sat 11–10 🚌 Free shuttle from major hotels ♿ Good 💷 Expensive

A sand craftsman in the Desert Conservation Reserve

IMG World of Adventure

Excursions

THE BASICS

➕ Off map to the south

Distance: From Dubai, traveling distance/time is 87 miles (140km)

Journey time: Around 90 minutes via the E11 Sheikh Zayed Road

Louvre Abu Dhabi
louvreabudhabi.ae
✉ Saadiyat Culturaal District

Sheikh Zayed Mosque
szgmc.gov.ae
✉ Off Sheikh Saeed bin Rashid St, Khor Al Maqta'a

Qasr Al Hosn
qasralhosn.ae
✉ Between Zayed the First Street and Khaled bin Al Waleed Street

Ferrari World
Ferrariworldabudhabi.com
✉ Yas Island

Warner Bros. World Abu Dhabi
wbworldabudhabi.com
✉ Yas Island

DID YOU KNOW?

● Abu Dhabi has 87% of all land in the UAE, with 26,000sq miles (67,340sq km)
● The population is 2.09 million, of which 551,000 are Emiratis

ABU DHABI

Capital of the UAE, Abu Dhabi has developed fast on the revenues from oil discovered in the 1970s. More conservative than Dubai, it has come late to mass tourism, but the capital, Abu Dhabi city, sitting on an island just off the coast, has developed a range of world-class attractions in the last decade. The first permanent structure in the city, Qasr Al Hosn, started in the 1760s as a watchtower but developed into a fort post 1795 and became the center of power for the Bani Yas tribe and subsequent sheikhs. Sheikh Zayed Mosque opened as a center of prayer and of cultural understanding; it is one of the world's largest, with a capacity of 50,000. Its graceful pillars, domes and minarets feature themes from around the Islamic world.

If you're an art lover you will soon have two amazing galleries to visit. The result of a cultural collaboration between France and the UAE, the Louvre Abu Dhabi opened in 2017 in a magnificent contemporary edifice designed by Jean Nouvel It features 300 major works from France's principal art museums in a changing program. Meanwhile the Guggenheim Abu Dhabi is currently in development in a futuristic Frank Gehry-designed building.

For those seeking action, Abu Dhabi hosts its own Formula 1 Grand Prix (Nov) and Ferrari World is a theme park branded by the Formula 1 racing team. Here you'll find the world's fastest roller coaster and the state-of-the-art Formula 1 simulator Scuderia Challenge. Opened in 2018, the covered theme park Warner Bros. Abu Dhabi has six zones and 29 attractions including rides and shows featuring all your favorite Warner Bros. characters.

HATTA

The mountain village of Hatta, less than 6 miles (10km) from the Oman border, is Dubai's oldest outpost. It's a popular spot for day-tripping Dubaians.

To reach it, simply follow Route 44 out of Dubai; it's about a 1.5-hour drive. The village is a relatively lush oasis among the dusty, serrated slopes of the Hajar Mountains, thanks in part to a dam in the hills above. There are few attractions in the center, apart from two watchtowers dating from 1880, but on the left of the first traffic circle as you enter the village is the Hatta Fort Hotel, an attractive, 50-suite hotel with restaurants, a golf course and a swimming pool. If you're not staying overnight here—and it is the only place to stay in Hatta—then at least pop in for a chilled drink. The information center in the lobby offers guided tours in 4x4 vehicles or maps and instructions if you're feeling confident enough to drive off-road yourself.

Hatta's main attraction is its position at the trailhead for off-road routes into the mountains. Hatta's rock pools—deep, dark pools surrounded by rocky outcrops—are just a short drive away. On the way you will pass the Hatta Heritage Village, which opened in 2001. This restored mountain village demonstrates how Emiratis survived in the mountains during the last century. A fort, built by Sheikh Maktoum bin Hashr Al Maktoum in 1896 to protect against raiders and invaders, is at its heart. The site itself dates back 2,000 to 3,000 years, but most buildings are no older than 200 years. Traditional building techniques were employed, using mud for the walls and palm fronds (*barasti*) for the roofs.

THE BASICS

✈ Off map to southwest

Distance: From Dubai, 90 miles (145km) via the E102; 70 miles (112km) via the E44

Journey time: 1.5 hours by car, 2 hours by bus (E16 from Al Sabkha bus station to Hatta Terminus—services every hour 6am–10pm)

🍴 Restaurant and café at Hatta Fort Hotel

♿ Few facilities

❓ Stay overnight to make the most of your visit. The Hatta Fort Hotel (tel: 809 9333, jaresorthotels.com) can organize guided trips to the pools and surrounding mountains.
The border with Oman runs through the Hajar Mountains, so carry your passport as proof of identity. If you travel by rental vehicle, check whether you are insured to travel into Oman. If not, travel to Hatta by the E102 route, which remains totally in Dubai territory.

Hatta Heritage Village

☎ 852 1374

🕐 Sat–Thu 8am–8.30pm, Fri 2.30–8.30

♿ Good 🚻 Free

Entertainment and Nightlife

MALLS

Out-of-town malls are growing in number. The newest of these is the nature-themed 350-store Cityland Mall (citylandmall.com), close to the site of the Global Village. A much more established mall is the 275-store, Arabic-themed Ibn Battuta Mall (ibnbattutamall.com) at Jebel Ali, on the way to Abu Dhabi, and Dubai Outlet Mall (dubaioutletmall.com) with 240 international names offering end-of-season style merchandise.

THE ADDRESS MONTGOMERIE GOLF COURSE

themontgomerie.com
This course, designed by Colin Montgomerie and Desmond Muirhead, offers tuition and training facilities, and the short game areas are floodlit.
➕ Off map ✉ Off Sheikh Zayed Road 5th interchange toward Emerald Hills ☎ 390 5600 ⏰ Daily 6am–9pm

AL HADHEERAH ARABIC EVENING

meydanhotels.com
Sit under the stars at this upscale desert camp for a spectacular Bedouin buffet. Price includes live entertainment, falcons, camel caravan and floorshow.
➕ Off map ✉ Bab Al Shams resort, off Sheikh Zayed Road interchange 4, inland on the Umm Suqeim Road ☎ 809 1694 ⏰ Dinner (reservations required)

AL SAHRA DESERT RESORT EQUESTRIAN CENTER

jaresortshotels.com
A canter among the dunes is a romantic fantasy, but it happens here.
➕ Off map ✉ Off the Al Ain Road Junction 29 on the Jebel Ali Road (E77) ☎ 427 4055 ⏰ Reservations required

DIVAZ ($$)

jaresortshotels.com
For a dinner to remember, head to this wooden dhow floating on Jebel Ali Marina. It offers an excellent set-price seafood buffet.
➕ Off map ✉ Jebel Ali Golf Resort, junction 13 Sheikh Zayed Road ☎ 814 5555 ⏰ Dinner

DUBAI AUTODROME/ KARTDROME

dubaiautodrome.com
An FIA-accredited track that offers a great range of high-octane rides, from racing Audi R8s to First Drive experiences (ages 12 and up). The kartdrome has indoor and outdoor tracks, with special sessions for kids (ages 7–12).
➕ Off map ✉ Dubai Sports City, off Sheikh Mohammed bin Zayed Road (E311) at Arabian Ranches Interchange ☎ 806 2220 ⏰ Reservations required

THE ELS CLUB

elsclubdubai.com
The Ernie Els-designed course ranges over 7,500 yards and has four tee sets. Each hole is designed to emulate an Els favorite on a classic course.
➕ Off map ✉ Dubai Sports City, off Sheikh Mohammed bin Zayed Road (E311) at Al Khail Road (E44) ☎ 425 1000 ⏰ Daily 6–6

GLOBAL VILLAGE

Operating only during the winter, this is said to be the world's largest leisure and entertainment complex, showcasing cultures from around the globe in a nightly carnival of entertainment, food and shopping on an immense scale.
➕ Off map ✉ Exit 37 Sheikh Mohammed bin Zayed Road ☎ 362 4112 ⏰ During festivals daily Sat–Wed 4pm–midnight, Thu–Fri 4pm–1am ♿ Good 💷 Inexpensive

Where to Stay

Dubai has unashamedly pitched itself as a luxury destination and its hotels are a big part of its appeal. Most hotels have been built since the start of the millennium, and older properties refubished, so amenities are modern and services excellent in all price brackets.

Introduction

The main question before you reserve your hotel is… do you want to spend the bulk of your time on the beach and do a little sightseeing, or do you want to spend your time exploring the city or shopping, with beach activities a low priority? You'll get excellent value for money at some of the 5-star and luxury boutique hotels if you choose to stay in the older districts of the city or out in the eastern suburbs. Conversely, you'll always pay a premium if you choose to stay on the coast.

There are more luxury hotels here than just about anywhere else in the world, which means at the top end of the market you'll be spoiled for choice. In the mid-range, Dubai has a variety in all areas of the city, from traditional low-rise guesthouses to high-rise towers. In the last decade the options for budget accommodations have improved dramatically. There is a catch, however. These budget hotels are often located in the new business districts rather than in the main tourist areas. It's a good idea to check what transport links are available before you reserve a room.

Room prices at the same hotel can vary enormously depending on whether there's a big convention in town or a major holiday. Prices are generally cheaper during the summer when the heat is oppressive, so that's the time to hunt for bargains. You can reserve all hotels through their own websites—and they'll advertise special rates here too—but it's always worth exploring booking sites for a better price.

TOURISM TAX

The Dubai government levies a tourist tax on room occupancy charged for every night of your stay. This ranges from 7 AED to 20 AED per room per night depending on the standard of your hotel. The tax is not included in the room rate (even when you use a booking site) and will be collected by your hotel, added to your bill at the end of your stay.

Budget Hotels

ARABIAN COURTYARD

arabiancourtyard.com

This long-standing Bur Dubai hotel abutting the Al Fahidi Historic District continues to be a popular choice for its location and range of amenities. There's a good-sized spa and pool complex, and the Sherlock Holmes Pub is a busy expat meeting spot.

➕ K3 ✉ Al Fahidi Street, Bur Dubai ☎ 351 9111 🚇 Al Fahidi

BEST WESTERN PREMIER DEIRA HOTEL

bestwesternpremierdubai.com

Set in a downtown neighborhood north of the creek, this is a well-appointed property with a health club and indoor pool, though it doesn't have the outside space of a resort hotel. There's easy access to the metro.

➕ N6 ✉ Corner of Abu Baker Al Siddique Road and Salah Al Din Road ☎ 5430 76108 🚇 Abu Baker Al Siddique

CITYMAX BUR DUBAI

citymaxhotels.com

A modern, functional and efficient 3-star hotel close to the historical sites. Rooms are small by Dubai standards, but the hotel has a good range of amenities including several restaurants, 24-hour room service, pool and gym.

➕ H4 ✉ Kuwait Street and Mankhool Road, Mankhool ☎ 407 8000 🚇 Al Fahidi

IBIS WORLD TRADE CENTER

ibis.com

The Ibis is hard to beat for economical accommodations. Rooms are clean, functional and comfortable, though not very spacious. Pleasing touches include Philippe Starck furniture and some stylish bars and restaurants.

➕ F5 ✉ World Trade Center, Sheikh Zayed Road ☎ 332 4444 🚇 Trade Center

ORIENT GUEST HOUSE

orientguesthouse.com

Traditional Arabic guesthouse with beautifully decorated rooms set around a shady courtyard in the heart of the Al Fahidi Historic District. Guests have access to the Arabian Courtyard hotel pool, steam room and gym.

➕ L4 ✉ Al Fahidi Historic District ☎ 351 9111 🚇 Al Fahidi

XVA HOTEL

xvahotel.com

This is the most unusual and stylish place to stay in Dubai. Set in a traditional building in Old Bastakiya (Al Fahidi Historic District), the individually styled rooms are set around three cool courtyards. Rooms are plush and individually designed, with numerous examples of art from the neighboring XVA Gallery. There's a rooftop terrace on which to watch the sunset and city lights.

➕ L4 ✉ Al Musalla–Al Fahidi roundabout, Al Fahidi Historic District ☎ 353 5383 🚇 Al Fahidi

AL FAHIDI HISTORIC DISTRICT

Though they have few of the facilities of modern-built hotels, the traditional guesthouses of the Al Fahidi Historic District are packed with atmosphere—XVA has a more "arty" decor, with Arabian Courtyard being uber-Arabic in design. Bur Dubai and Deira are both bustling districts in the evenings, the souks are especially lively, and everything is easily explored on foot from here.

Mid-Range Hotels

THE ADDRESS MONTGOMERIE DUBAI

theaddress.com

Set among the well-groomed greens of the Colin Montgomerie-designed championship golf course (▷ 106), this boutique hotel has sumptuously furnished rooms, an excellent spa and a gourmet restaurant. It's a short ride away from the razzmatazz of the city.

➕ Off map ✉ Emirates Hills ☎ 390 5600

CROWNE PLAZA SHEIKH ZAYED ROAD

crowneplaza.com

Most of the hotels on this stretch of Sheikh Zayed Road are geared toward business travelers, but the Crowne Plaza makes a play for holidaymakers with competitive pricing and a range of down-to-earth bars and restaurants.

➕ D–E5 ✉ Sheikh Zayed Road ☎ 331 1111 🚇 Emirates Towers

DUKES DUBAI

dukesdubai.com

Sister hotel of Dukes of Mayfair, London, and sitting on the seafront on the main trunk section of Palm Jumeirah, Dukes has quality decor and a good range of facilities including an indoor pool.

➕ b1 ✉ Oceana, Palm Jumeirah ☎ 4455 1111 🚇 Palm Monorail

FOUR POINTS BY SHERATON BUR DUBAI

sheraton.com

You can't beat the location of this mid-range small Starwood hotel; Al Fahidi Historic District and BurJuman are within walking distance. With just 125 rooms, the Four Points attracts a mix of business and leisure travelers. Facilities include a fitness center and pool, as well as five restaurant options.

➕ K4 ✉ Khalid bin Walid Street ☎ 397 7444 🚇 Al Fahidi

GROSVENOR HOUSE

grosvenorhouse-dubai.com

The first hotel to be completed in the burgeoning marina development is a tapering 45-story tower. Facilities are state-of-the-art with a particularly strong lineup of restaurants and bars.

➕ a1 ✉ West Marina Beach, Sheikh Zayed Road ☎ 399 8888 🚋 Tram: Jumeirah Beach Residence 1

THE H DUBAI

hhoteldubai.com

One of the best priced of the quality hotels in this neighborhood of Dubai, with no less than 11 bars and eateries on site. The high-rise H Dubai caters well to both tourist and business guests.

➕ F5 ✉ Sheikh Zayed Road ☎ 501 8888 🚇 World Trade Center

HILTON DUBAI CREEK

hilton.com

A modernist's dream, the boutique Hilton Dubai Creek has architecture by Uruguayan architect Carlos Ott. A riot of glass and steel inside, bedrooms have dramatic black-and-white bathrooms and service is personal and professional.

➕ L6 ✉ Baniyas Road ☎ 227 1111

INTERCONTINENTAL DUBAI FESTIVAL CITY

ichotels.com

The Intercontinental rises high over the eastern reaches of Dubai Creek,

surrounded by the shopping and entertainment of Festival City and close to the Yacht Club and Golf Course. Interior styling is understated by Dubai standards, but still refined and comfortable.

🔲 Off map ✉ Dubai Festival City ☎ 701 1111

MELIA DESERT PALM

melia.com

Set out in a new district east of Dubai Creek, this well-priced spa retreat offers luxurious rooms in a true tropical oasis. With Bang and Olufsen sound systems and iPods in the rooms, they are well equipped too. Amenities include spa, fitness center and horse-riding school.

🔲 Off map ✉ Warsan 2 ☎ 323 8888

OASIS BEACH TOWER

jaresorts.com

This high-rise tower on Dubai Marina offers large serviced apartments, great for families and groups. It sits conveniently above The Walk, with its range of shops and eateries. There's a private pool deck on site and guests have access to the private beach of the Jebel Ali Golf Resort, a shuttle bus ride away.

🔲 a1 ✉ Dubai Marina ☎ 399 4444 🚋 Tram: Jumeirah Beach Residence 1

PARK HYATT DUBAI

hyatt.com

Next to the Dubai Creek Golf Course, this 5-star property is a haven of tranquility within the downtown area. The whitewashed low-rise buildings set in lush gardens offer a total contrast to the many high-rise hotel towers. Rooms are relatively minimalist, yet chic.

🔲 L8 ✉ Dubai Creek Club St ☎ 602 1234

RADISSON BLU RESIDENCE DUBAI MARINA

radissonblu.com

This high-rise apart-hotel property in Dubai Marina offers superb views and rooms have full-sized glass doors onto the balcony for guests to get the benefit. The contemporary decor is by well-known interior designer Matteo Nunziati.

🔲 a2 ✉ Street K, Dubai Marina ☎ 435 5000 🚋 Tram: Dubai Marina

TOWERS ROTANA

rotana.com

In the heart of the action on Sheikh Zayed Road, Towers offers stylish high-rise accommodations. There are several room types, with the Classic being compact. Long's Bar Pub is a popular after-work and weekend meeting place.

🔲 C5 ✉ Sheikh Zayed Road ☎ 343 8000 🚇 Emirates Towers

VIDA DOWNTOWN

vida-hotels.com

An ultra-contemporary six-story Arabian-styled hotel in the shadow of Burj Khalifa. Rooms are cool and neutral, and are well equipped. There are three restaurants on site, plus a pool and fitness center, and a free shuttle to take you to The Dubai Mall.

🔲 A7 ✉ The Old Town, Downtown Dubai ☎ 428 6888

HOTEL DESIGN

There is no greater concentration of luxury hotels in the world than in Dubai, but interiors, particularly, can be over-the-top—the interior of the Burj Al Arab (▷ 112) is a prime example. However, chic minimalism isn't unknown here: the Park Hyatt Dubai (▷ left), and the Armani Hotel (▷ 112) are hotels that prove less is more.

Luxury Hotels

PRICES

Expect to pay over 1,500 AED for a double room in a luxury hotel

ARMANI HOTEL

armanihotels.com

Burj Khalifa's boutique property is certainly impressive. Styled by fashion designer Giorgio Armani, every aspect displays his touch. There's an Armani shop on site, along with eight restaurants and a large spa with outdoor pool.

✚ B6 ✉ Burj Khalifa, Sheikh Zayed Road ☎ 888 3888 🚇 Dubai Mall

BURJ AL ARAB

jumeirah.com

While the exterior styling has graceful lines, the interior is unashamedly lavish and recently refurbished. The accommodations are suite only, each across two floors and decorated in extravagant style. All suites come with a personal butler service.

✚ e1 ✉ Jumeirah ☎ 301 7777

JUMEIRAH BEACH HOTEL

jumeirahbeachhotel.com

On the north side of the Burj Al Arab, the wave-shaped Jumeirah Beach Hotel is a vast, luxurious resort, newly renovated and popular with families thanks to its range of sports and leisure amenities and its proximity to the Wild Wadi waterpark (▷ 94).

✚ e1 ✉ Beach Road ☎ 348 0000

THE OBEROI

oberoihotels.com

The Oberoi offers unashamed modern luxury with international appeal. It offers several quality restaurants, the trendy Iris lounge, and a large spa with an indoor infinity pool.

✚ Off map ✉ Oberoi Center, Business Bay ☎ 444 1444 🚇 Business Bay

ONE&ONLY ROYAL MIRAGE

oneandonlyresorts.com

The exclusive One&Only resort has three different areas of accommodations. Set in 65 acres (26ha) and with a long stretch of beachfront, it feels expansive and exclusive. The KidsOnly activity program makes families very welcome.

✚ b1 ✉ Al Sufouh Road ☎ 399 9999 🚊 Tram: Media City or Palm Jumeirah

RAFFLES DUBAI

raffles.com

The towering glass pyramid of Raffles Dubai is an unforgettable sight, especially at night. Inside, it's beautifully appointed throughout, with five restaurants and bars. There's a PlayZone for kids, an outdoor pool, plus a spa and, most unusually, a rooftop Zen garden.

✚ H8 ✉ Wafi City Mall, Oud Metha ☎ 324 8888 🚇 Dubai Healthcare City

SHANGRI-LA

shangri-la.com

This 41-story celeb-haunt has sumptuous bedrooms—press a button and your room's curtains will open to reveal one of the best views of Sheikh Zayed Road.

✚ C5 ✉ Sheikh Zayed Road ☎ 343 8888 🚇 Emirates Towers

WALDORF ASTORIA DUBAI PALM JUMEIRAH

hilton.com

A low-rise resort stretching on an expanse of private beach with large pools, this is a luxurious retreat with a large spa and six eateries.

✚ d1 ✉ Crescent Road, The Palm ☎ 818 2222

Need to Know

This section is packed with practical information to make the most of your trip to Dubai, from helpful advice when you first arrive to getting around during your stay, plus useful websites.

Planning Ahead

When to Go

The best time to visit Dubai is in the cooler months from October to May. Year-round temperatures are hot, but summers are incredibly hot. There are several major festivals, sporting events and exhibitions throughout the year when hotel rooms are at a premium.

TIME
Dubai is 4 hours ahead of GMT, 9 hours ahead of New York (8 hours during Daylight Savings Time) and 3 hours behind Singapore.

AVERAGE DAILY MAXIMUM TEMPERATURES											
JAN	FEB	MAR	APR	MAY	JUN	JUL	AUG	SEP	OCT	NOV	DEC
66°F	66°F	72°F	77°F	81°F	90°F	95°F	95°F	90°F	86°F	77°F	66°F
19°C	19°C	22°C	25°C	27°C	32°C	35°C	35°C	32°C	30°C	25°C	19°C

April–October The summer is extremely hot and dry; any outdoor activity is discouraged.
November–December Temperatures drop a little and Dubai's outdoor season of sports and café society starts.
January–March Temperatures are similar to November–December but with a chance of short, sharp rainstorms, which can result in flooded roads and leaking roofs.

WHAT'S ON

January
Dubai Shopping Festival (can run into Feb): Shops discount stock by up to 80 percent. Events include outdoor music shows and children's activities.
February
Omega Dubai Desert Classic: Usually takes place at the Emirates Golf Club. It has been part of Europe's PGA Tour since 1989.
Dubai Duty Free Tennis Championships: Held at the Dubai Tennis Stadium on Garhoud Road, this ATP tournament features all the top seeds.

Dubai International Jazz Festival: A diverse selection of performers is booked for the three-night festival.
March
Dubai International Boat Show: Your chance to see some of the world's most expensive yachts and cruisers in close-up at the Dubai International Marine Club in Mina Seyahi.
Dubai World Cup: The world's richest horse race, at the Meydan racecourse. The World Cup race itself, always held on a Saturday, is the climax of the Dubai Racing Carnival.

May
Dubai Traditional Dhow Races: The six-race series concludes in June.
June–August
Dubai Summer Surprises: A reprise of the January shopping festival.
December
Dubai International Film Festival: Inaugurated in 2004, the festival is gaining in popularity every year.
Emirates Airlines Dubai Rugby Sevens: A seven-a-side rugby tournament when Dubai's expats come out to play.

Dubai Online

visitdubai.com
The official website for the Department of Tourism and Commerce Marketing, with comprehensive information for those visiting, living or doing business in Dubai.

dubaicalendar.ae
The official "What's on When" website with a full listing of concerts, festivals, sporting events and exhibitions listed by month with connections to official websites.

dubaiculture.gov.ae
Dubai Culture and Arts Authority's website has information on Dubai heritage and the wide-ranging cultural scene, including traditional Arabian and contemporary art.

guide2dubai.com
Information for visitors and prospective foreign workers, with lots of practical background on customs and lifestyle.

uaeinteract.com
A wealth of background information about Dubai and the other emirates of the UAE including economic news, politics and government.

dubai.com
Easy-to-use information and booking site, with sections on hotels, attractions and restaurants.

thenational.ae
Dubai's oldest English-language press source can still be found in print but has excellent online info, including a "What's on" section covering the coming weekend.

whatson.ae
An excellent site for those living and visiting Dubai with sections on sport, nightlife and new restaurant openings across the UAE.

TRAVEL SITE

fodors.com
A complete travel-planning site. You can research prices and weather, reserve air tickets, cars and rooms, ask questions (and get answers) from fellow travelers, and find links to other sites.

INTERNET ACCESS

All hotels offer internet access, with most having free WiFi throughout the property. The two telecom providers have WiFi hotspots throughout the city at shopping malls and cafés, but they are not free and you require a local SIM card to access the service. Etisalat (etisalat.ae) offers three visitor line products for AED100 which offer various call, surf and text packages. These are all valid for 14 days.
Du (du.ae) offers a Tourist Plan and you can reserve your Tourist Sim before you arrive (cost 65AED).

Getting There

ENTRY REQUIREMENTS

● Passport holders of the following countries will be issued with a free visit visa on arrival in Dubai: UK and member states of the EU, Republic of Ireland, US, Australia, Canada.

● Free visas for the USA and UK are valid for 30 days and can be renewed once if you wish to extend your stay (toll-free 24-hours AMER—General Directorate of Residency and Foreigners Affairs—tel: 8005111 for information about visas).

● Other nationalities should consult the embassy of the UAE in their own countries as visa rules are complex and will require you to pay a fee.

● Passport and visa regulations can change without warning, so always check before you travel.

AIRPORTS

Dubai International Airport (DXB) is on the Deira side of the creek, about 3 miles (5km) from the center. One of the busiest airports in the world, it's very well equipped. Flights take around 7 hours from Western Europe and 17 hours from New York. A second airport, Dubai World Central—Al Maktoum International Airport (DWC), opened in 2013, though far fewer carriers fly there at present.

FROM DUBAI INTERNATIONAL AIRPORT

Transfers to all parts of the city are short, with a 10-minute journey by car into Deira and 40–50 minutes to Dubai Marina and the coastal resorts.

DUBAI METRO

● There are Metro stations at Terminal 1 and Terminal 3 of Dubai International Airport for easy access to Deira, Bur Dubai and down along Sheikh Zayed Road (a shuttle bus links Terminal 2 to Terminal 1 for access to the Metro system). If your hotel is close to a Metro station it's a quick transfer.

● You'll need to buy a Nol travel pass, 10-journey travel ticket or a day ticket before you enter the Metro system (see Getting Around). There are ticket offices and automatic machines at each terminal. Normal operating hours for the Metro are Sat–Wed 5am–midnight, Thu 5am–1am, Fri 10am–1am. Trains run every 4 minutes at peak times, and every 7 off peak.

● Metro rules allow two suitcases/bags per traveler and these should be stored in the designated areas. Alcohol is not allowed on the Metro system.

BUS SERVICES
Few bus services stop at the Dubai International Airport and most feed other bus stations for transfer to outlying districts. They are not as useful or as quick as other forms of transport from the airport.

TAXI
Taxis are the most efficient way to get from the airport to your hotel and there are stands outside each terminal and any lines that form usually move quickly, even at peak times. Taxis are metered and fares from the airport start at 25 AED, with increments of 1.96 AED per 0.6 miles (1km) between 6am and 10pm (fares rise between 10pm and 6am). Sample fares and travel times are as follows:
● Airport to Jumeirah Beach Hotel: 63 AED and 30 minutes
● Airport to Atlantis, The Palm: 87 AED and 40 minutes
● Airport to Bur Dubai: 45 AED and 20 minutes
For further information visit dubaitaxi.ae.

CAR RENTAL
Traffic is dense, the road layout is confusing, road conditions are variable and driving standards are poor. As a result it's not advisable to rent a car unless you are a confident and experienced driver.

HOTEL TRANSFER
Many hotels have transfer facilities and will have a car waiting for you at the airport. Make inquiries when you reserve your room.

VACCINATIONS
There are no vaccinations needed for entering Dubai. This information can change so check before you travel.

INSURANCE

Before you travel, make sure you have insurance cover for travel delays and lost/stolen belongings. Check your home policy or bank/credit card policies as these may come as standard. Otherwise buy a stand-alone policy.
It's also vital to have insurance to cover medical expenses because, aside from emergency treatment, you'll need to pay for any medical treatment you need and fees are high.

INFORMATION

For airport inquiries: Dubai
☎ 224 5555
dubaiairports.com

EMERGENCIES

Police: Emergency number ☎ 999, call center for inquiries ☎ 901

Getting Around

TRAM AND MONOROIL

- A tram service (5am–1am) links Damac and Dubai Multi Commodities Centre (DMCC) Metro stations with 11 stations around Dubai Marina.
- A monorail service runs along the spine of Palm Jumeirah.

ABRAS AND WATER TAXIS

- There are water taxi services serving Dubai Creek and the Dubai Marina/Palm Jumeirah areas.
- The traditional wooden *abras* cross between Deira and Bur Dubai on two routes between the north and south shores. Price per crossing is 1 AED for the standard *abra*, 2 AED for the air-conditioned *abra*.
- Dubai Ferry operates along Dubai Creek and the extended Dubai Canal inland of Downtown Dubai with an outlet into the sea along the Jumeirah coastline. Prices range from 50 AED–75 AED per one-way trip. For timetable see rta.ae.
- Luxurious water taxis are available (daily 10–10) for transfers between Dubai Creek and Dubai Marina, with 61 stations in all. These must be reserved in advance, tel: 800 9090.

PUBLIC TRANSPORT

- Dubai has an integrated public transport system with two Metro lines, a network of feeder buses and one tram service linking Metro stations with nearby residential neighborhoods.
- Tickets are valid across the system, with transfers being allowed within the maximum ticket journey times.
- Dubai is divided into seven transport zones and fares are tiered depending on how many zones you travel across, from T1 to T3.
- Journey costs are deducted electronically as you enter and leave the stations or the bus by touching the card against the electronic card readers. For further information visit nol.ae.
- There are ticket offices at the airport and main stations and vending machines at bus and Metro stations. Passes can be topped up online.
- For more information visit rta.ae or tel: 800 90 90.

Types of Ticket

- You must buy a prepaid Nol ticket/card.
- The maximum daily cost for all standard travel throughout the system is 20 AED.
- The Nol Silver Card costs 25 AED (with a 19 AED credit to get you started) and can be topped up regularly. It is valid for five years.
- The Nol Red Ticket is a paper pass that carries credit for ten journeys of your choice. The pass costs 2 AED plus the cost of the journeys and is valid for the ten trips or a maximum of 90 days.
- A paper day ticket costs 2 AED for the ticket and 20 AED for the travel.

Zone Charges

- Charges are T1 zone (same zone or crossing into next zone on journey less than 3km) Nol Silver Card 3 AED; Nol Red Card 4 AED. T2 zone (crossing zones) Nol Silver Card 5 AED, Red Card 6 AED. T3 zone (three or more zones) Nol Silver Card 7.5 AED, Red Card 8.5 AED.
- T1 rides are valid for 90 minutes with no connections; T1–T3 are valid for 180 minutes including connections.

DUBAI METRO

● The Dubai Metro has two lines. The Red Line runs from the airport into Deira under Dubai Creek and along Sheik Zayed Road to Jebel Ali. The Green Line links neighborhoods north and east of Deira with neighborhoods south of Dubai Creek in Bur Dubai.
● There are two crossover stations: Union in Deira and BurJuman in Bur Dubai.
● Normal operating hours are Sat–Wed 5am–midnight, Thu 5am–1am, Fri 10am–1am, the Green line opens a little later at 5.30am. Trains run every 4 minutes at peak times.

BUSES

● The bus service is designed to link residential and tourist neighborhoods with the Metro system and buses run regularly on set routes.
● Bus stops are covered and air-conditioned.
● The most useful services for visitors are those that link the resorts on the coast at Jumeirah, Dubai Marina and Jebel Ali to the Red Line for quick access to the attractions of Sheikh Zayed Road, and the Deira and Bur Dubai districts.

TAXIS

● Taxis are plentiful (over 7,000 in the city) and cheap, though driver skill levels vary.
● Taxis are metered. Minimum fare is 10 AED around town, 25 AED from the airport. Meter starter fare is 5 AED if hailed on the roadside, 10–12 AED if dispatched. Metered fare is then 1.96 AED per 1km (0.6 miles). Fares rise between 10pm and 6am.
● Taxis can also be booked by the morning or the day to make sightseeing easier.
● Taxis will wait outside all hotels, tourist landmarks and malls.
● Pink-topped taxis cater to women and families only.
● For further information visit dtc.dubai.ae. The central number for taxi booking 24 hours per day is 0420 80808.
● Rounding up the fare to the nearest 5 AED as a tip for the driver is normal practice.

Essential Facts

TOURIST BOARD

Dubai Department of Tourism and Commerce Marketing operates information offices at the airport (24-hours) and in all the major malls (operating mall hours). The department does have a comprehensive website (dubaitourism.ae) and an app, so you can create your ideal itinerary before you travel and access information on the move.

Head Office in Dubai

✉ Al Fattan Plaza, Airport Road, Deira ☎ 600 555559

Overseas offices in the UK

✉ 4th Floor, Nuffield House, 41–46 Piccadilly, London W1J 0DS ☎ 020 7321 6110

ETIQUETTE

Dubai is one of the most liberal destinations in the Muslim Middle East but certain aspects of behavior could cause offence, and in some cases result in arrest. It would be respectful not to:

● wear clothing that reveals a lot of bare flesh
● indulge in public displays of affection such as kisses (even hand-holding may be frowned upon)
● get intoxicated

ELECTRICITY

● The electrical current is 220/240 volts and 50 cycles. Plugs are the three-prong type, the same as the UK. Americans will need a transformer to power equipment.

MEDICAL TREATMENT

● The quality of medical treatment in Dubai is high, with well-qualified English-speaking staff.
● Some hotels have a doctor on call and a list of dental clinics.
● Emergency treatment is free but the cost of other treatment is high.
● You will be asked to provide proof you can pay before treatment begins.
● Full health insurance is strongly advised.
● The two main government hospitals are Dubai Hospital tel: 219 5000 in Deira and Rashid Hospital tel: 800 342 in Oud Metha.
● The private American Hospital (tel: 336 7777) is also in Oud Metha.
● All three hospitals have emergency departments.
● Pharmacies are well stocked and will sell many products without prescription.

MONEY MATTERS

● You can change money at the airport, at banks and at hotels.
● You'll find numerous ATMs throughout the city, in shopping malls and in hotel lobbies.
● Credit cards are widely accepted. Some smaller retailers may levy an extra charge on cards, though they may give you a discount for paying in cash.
● Haggling is expected in souks and markets but malls tend to have fixed prices.
● Traveler's checks cannot be used to pay for goods in Dubai. They can be cashed at banks, exchange centers and hotels.

OPENING HOURS

● Friday is the holy day in the Muslim world so the weekend is typically Fri–Sat, though some businesses close Thu–Fri.

- Shopping malls open daily 10am–midnight, other shops usually 9am–1pm and 4pm–9pm. All shops close on Friday between 11.30am and 1.30pm for the main prayer gathering of the week.
- Government offices are open Sun–Thu 7.30am–2.30pm.
- Post offices are open Sun–Thu 8am–1pm and 4pm–7pm.
- Commercial businesses open Sun–Thu 8am–5pm.
- Banks open Sat–Wed 8am–1pm and Thu 8am–noon.
- Many restaurants serve throughout the day, though some are only open in the evenings.
- During Ramadan many restaurants only open after sunset.

PUBLIC HOLIDAYS

All the major Muslim celebrations change date each year in line with the lunar calendar.

Moveable holidays:
- Eid Al Adha (Feast of the Sacrifice at the end of the *hajj* pilgrimage to Mecca)
- Ras Al-Sana (Islamic New Year)
- Mawlid Al-Nabi (the Prophet Mohammed's Birthday)
- Lailat Al Mi'Raj (Ascension of the Prophet Mohammed)
- Eid Al Fitr (three-day celebration to mark the end of Ramadan)

Fixed-date holidays:
- New Year's Day (1 Jan)
- Ascension to the throne of Sheikh Zayed (6 Aug)
- UAE National Day (2 Dec)

SENSIBLE PRECAUTIONS

- Don't carry large amounts of cash and leave valuables in the hotel safe.
- Women travelers have few worries about harassment, but may be subject to unwanted attention if wearing swimwear on beaches.

EMBASSIES AND CONSULATES

- UK
- ✉ Al Seef Road, Bur Dubai
- ☎ 309 4444 🕐 Sun–Thu 7.30am–2.30pm
- USA
- ✉ Corner of Al Seef Road and Sheikh Khalifa bin Zayed Road, Bur Dubai ☎ 309 4000
- 🕐 By appointment only. Telephone for appointment Sun–Thu 8am–10am
- Germany
- ✉ Jumeirah 1, Street 14A
- ☎ 349 8888 🕐 Sun–Thu 9am–12pm
- France
- ✉ 32nd Floor, Habtoor Business Tower, Dubai Marina
- ☎ 408 4900 🕐 Daily 8.30am–12.30am
- Spain
- Embassy in Abu Dhabi
- ✉ Al Nayman Building 96, Al Ladeem Street ☎ 2 407 9000 626 9544 🕐 Mon–Thu 9am–1pm

MONEY

The unit of currency in Dubai (and the other emirates of the United Arab Emirates) is the Emirati Dirham (AED or Dh). It is linked to the dollar at an exchange rate of 3.67 AED to 1$. Each Dirham is divided into 100 fils.

Language

The official language in Dubai is Arabic, but English is widely spoken. People are always happy, and proud, to practice their foreign languages, but even if you only speak a few words of Arabic, you will generally meet with an enthusiastic response. The following is a phonetic transliteration from the Arabic script. Words or letters in brackets indicate the different form that is required when addressing, or speaking as, a woman. All road signs and direction markers and all signage at airport terminals and on public transport are in both Arabic and English.

USEFUL WORDS AND PHRASES	
yes	*naam*
no	*laa*
please	*min fadlak (min fadlik)*
thank you	*shukran*
you're welcome	*afwan*
hello *(to Muslims)*	*as-salamu alaykum*
response	*wa-alaykum as-salam*
hello *(to Copts)*	*as-salamu lakum*
welcome	*ahlan wa-sahlan*
response	*ahlan bika (ahlan biki)*
goodbye	*ma-asalama*
good morning	*sabaah al-khayr*
response	*sabaah an-nuur*
good evening	*masaa al-khayr*
response	*masaa an-nuur*
how are you?	*kayfa haalak (kayfa haalik)*
fine, thank you	*bikhayr, shukran*
God willing	*In shaa al-laah*
no problem	*laa toojad mushkilah*
sorry	*aasif (aasifa)*
excuse me	*an idhnak (an idhnik)*
my name is…	*ismii…*
do you speak English?	*hal tatakallam al-inglizyah? (hal tatakallamin…)*
I don't understand	*laa afhami*
I understand	*afhami*
I don't speak Arabic	*Arabiclaa atakallam al-arabiyyah*
help!	*tarri!*
thief!	*an-najdah!*
police	*liss*
go away	*ab-eed (ab-eedy)*

MONEY	
money	*niqood*
where is the bank?	*ayna al-bank?*
dirham	*dirham*
half a pound	*nisf junaih*
small change	*fakkah*
post office	*maktab al-bareed*
mail	*bareed*
check	*sheak*
traveler's check	*sheak siyahi*
credit card	*man*

RESTAURANT	
restaurant	*mataami*
I would like	*oreed an aakul*
alcohol/beer	*beerah*
coffee/tea	*qahwah/shaay*
mineral water	*meeyah maadaniah*
milk	*haleeb*
red wine/white wine	*nabeez ahmar/abyadd*
bread	*khoubz*
salt and pepper	*milh wa filfil*
meat	*lahm*
breakfast	*ifttar*
lunch	*ghadaa*
dinner	*aashaa*
table	*maaida*
waiter	*nadil*
menu	*qaaimat at-ttaam*
bill	*fatourah*

TRAVEL	
I'm lost	*ana taaih (ana taaiha)*
where is…?	*ayna…?*
airport	*mattar*
boat	*markib*
bus	*baass*
street	*shaari*
taxi rank	*mawqif at-taxi*
train	*qitar*
train station	*mahatat al-qitar*
left/right	*yassar/yameen*
straight on	*ala tuul*
return ticket	*tadhkarah zihaab wa rigooa*
car	*sayarah*
passport	*jawaz as-safar*

Timeline

1820 Britain signs an agreement with tribal leaders along the Gulf Coast. The British Navy protects the coast from pirates in return for a degree of influence in local affairs.

1833 The Al Maktoum branch of the Bani Yas tribal group relocates from farther up the coast to the area surrounding Dubai Creek.

1892 Individual states—including Dubai—sign agreements with Britain to manage their internal affairs while Britain deals with foreign matters. The Maktoum family adopts a progressive trading policy, abolishing commercial taxes.

1912 Sheikh Saeed bin Maktoum Al Maktoum takes control of Dubai.

1950s Oil is discovered in the Gulf.

1952 The seven ruling families of the region, the emirates, form the Trucial Council—the first formal, political bond between the city states.

1958 Sheikh Rashid bin Saeed Al Maktoum becomes Dubai's ruler. Knowing Dubai's oil supplies are limited, his economic strategy is based on attracting more trade and tourism.

1959 Sheikh Rashid orders the construction of Dubai's first airport.

1960 Dubai's creek is dredged at a cost of $850,000. This allows huge cargo ships that can't dock in Abu Dhabi to offload the equipment for the oil industry infrastructure.

1971 The seven emirates gain independence from Britain and form the United Arab Emirates, led by Abu Dhabi's Sheikh Zayed bin Sultan Al Nahyan.

1972 Port Rashid, Dubai's deep-water harbor, opens. Business soon floods into the new port, in part due to tensions between Iraq and Iran.

1979 Sheikh Rashid becomes president of the UAE. Dubai's first skyscraper, the Dubai World Trade Center, is opened.

1985 Dubai's new airline, Emirates, is based at Dubai International Airport. Jebel Ali Free Zone is founded, based around Dubai's second deep-water port, Jebel Ali, the world's largest artificial harbor.

1990 Sheikh Rashid dies and is succeeded by his son, Sheikh Maktoum bin Rashid Al Maktoum.

1996 The first Dubai World Cup horse race is run, with the richest prize purse in the world.

1999 The high-tech Burj Al Arab hotel is opened.

2002 Non-nationals are allowed to own property in Dubai freehold.

2003 Ground is broken on the Dubai Marina and The World projects.

2008 Atlantis, The Palm hotel on Palm Jumeirah hosts a spectacular opening party.

late 2008 The financial crisis rocks Dubai, bringing sudden and dramatic change. New developments are put on hold and existing developments are stopped mid-construction.

2009 Dubai Metro system opens.

2010 Burj Khalifa, currently the world's tallest tower, is officially opened.

2018 The UAE introduces Value Added Tax (VAT) on purchases, set at 5%. This reverses over a century of tax-free trading in Dubai

2020 Dubai will host Expo 2020; six months of attractions, experiences and pavilions celebrating global innovation, collaboration and creativity.

SHEIKH RASHID BIN SAEED AL MAKTOUM

Father of the current sheikh, Rashid (1912–1990) oversaw several high-profile civil works that transformed Dubai from a locally important trading town into a regional commercial hub. Though he reigned from 1958, it was after independence in the 1970s that Rashid's vision for Dubai began to bear fruit. The airport came on line, Port Rashid commercial harbor opened on the coast, Dubai Creek was dredged a second time to allow bigger vessels to enter, Al Shindagha road tunnel connected the north and south banks of the creek, and Dubai dry docks welcomed marine building and repair work from around the world. These investments brought commercial success and in turn allowed Dubai to invest in the expansive schemes of the present regime.

Index

CityPack Dubai

Published by AA Publishing, a trading name of AA Media Limited, whose registered office is Fanum House, Basing View, Basingstoke, Hampshire RG21 4EA. Registered number 06112600.

Written and updated by Lindsay Bennett
Series editor Clare Ashton
Design work Liz Baldin
Colour reprographics Ian Little

Printed and bound in China by 1010 Printing Group Limited

A CIP catalogue record for this book is available from the British Library.

ISBN 978-0-7495-8175-6

A05671
Maps in this title produced from mapping data supplied by Global Mapping, Brackley, UK © Global Mapping and data available from openstreetmap.org © under the Open Database License found at opendatacommons.org
Transport map © Communicarta Ltd, UK

Titles in the Series

- Amsterdam
- Bangkok
- Barcelona
- Berlin
- Boston
- Brussels & Bruges
- Budapest
- Dubai
- Dublin
- Edinburgh
- Florence
- Hong Kong
- Istanbul
- Krakow
- Las Vegas
- Lisbon
- London
- Madrid
- Milan
- Munich
- New York
- Orlando
- Paris
- Prague
- Rome
- San Francisco
- Shanghai
- Singapore
- Sydney
- Toronto
- Venice
- Vienna
- Washington

We would like to thank the following photographers, companies and picture libraries for their assistance in the preparation of this book.

2 AA/C Sawyer; 3 AA/C Sawyer; 4–18t AA/C Sawyer; 5 Urbanmyth/Alamy Stock Photo Stock Photo; 6cl AA/C Sawyer; 6c Burj Khalifa; 6cr AA/C Sawyer; 6bl Hannu Liivaar/Alamy Stock Photo; 6bc AA/C Sawyer; 6br Level 43 Bar; 7l AA/C Sawyer; 7c Viacheslav Khmelnytskyi/Alamy Stock Photo; 7r AA/C Sawyer; 7bl AA/C Sawyer; 7bc Meraas.com; 7br AA/C Sawyer; 10-11ct AA/C Sawyer; 10 AA/C Sawyer; 10–11c AA/C Sawyer; 10–11cb AA/C Sawyer; 11 AA/C Sawyer; 13t Madinat Jumeirah; 13c Madinat Jumeirah; 13b AA/C Sawyer; 14ct Hoi An Restaurant, Shangri-La Hotel; 14cb AA/C Sawyer; 14b Courtesy of Atlantis The Palm, Dubai; 16ct Courtesy of Atlantis The Palm, Dubai; 16cb IKandy, Shangri-La Hotel; 16b Madinat Jumeirah; 17ct Raffles, Dubai; 17c Courtesy of Atlantis The Palm, Dubai; 17cb AA/C Sawyer; 17b AA/C Sawyer; 18ct Address Hotel; 18c imageBROKER/Alamy Stock Photo; 18br Courtesy of Atlantis The Palm, Dubai; 19 AA/C Sawyer; 20 AA/C Sawyer; 24l AA/C Sawyer; 24r AA/C Sawyer; 25l AA/C Sawyer; 25c AA/C Sawyer; 25r AA/C Sawyer; 26l AA/C Sawyer; 26r AA/C Sawyer; 27l AA/C Sawyer; 27c AA/C Sawyer; 27r AA/C Sawyer; 28l Hemis/Alamy Stock Photo; 28c Megapress/Alamy Stock Photo; 28r Megapress/Alamy Stock Photo; 29l QE2; 29r QE2; 30l Yvette Cardozo/Alamy Stock Photo; 30c Yvette Cardozo/Alamy Stock Photo; 30r Tibor Bognar/Alamy Stock Photo; 31l imageBROKER/Alamy Stock Photo; 31c AA/C Sawyer; 31r AA/C Sawyer; 32l AA/C Sawyer; 32tr AA/C Sawyer; 32br AA/C Sawyer; 33 AA/C Sawyer; 34-38t AA/C Sawyer; 34bl Alserkal Cultural Foundation; 34br John Kellerman/Alamy Stock Photo; 35 Megapress/Alamy Stock Photo; 36bl PhotoDreams/Alamy Stock Photo; 36br The Majlis Gallery; 37 AA/C Sawyer; 39–40t AA/C Sawyer; 41–42t AA/C Sawyer; 42c–44t AA/C Sawyer; 45 AA/C Sawyer; 48l AA/C Sawyer; 48c AA/C Sawyer; 48r AA/C Sawyer; 49l AA/C Sawyer; 49c AA/C Sawyer; 49r AA/C Sawyer; 50l AA/C Sawyer; 50r AA/C Sawyer; 51l AA/C Sawyer; 51r AA/C Sawyer; 51cl AA/C Sawyer; 52l AA/C Sawyer; 52r AA/C Sawyer; 53-54t Art Directors & TRIP/Alamy Stock Photo; 53b Art Directors & TRIP/Alamy Stock Photo; 54bl Women's Museum; 55t AA/C Sawyer; 56 AA/C Sawyer; 57t–58t AA/C Sawyer; 59 Mathias Beinling/Alamy Stock Photo; 62tl Burj Khalifa; 62cl Burj Khalifa; 62cr Julija/Stockimo/Alamy Stock Photo; 63 Burj Khalifa; 64l Iain Masterton/Alamy Stock Photo; 64r Dubai Aquarium & Underwater Zoo; 65l Hannu Liivaar/Alamy Stock Photo; 65r Kumar Sriskandan/Alamy Stock Photo; 66t Dubai Frame/Dubai Municipality; 66c Dubai Frame/Dubai Municipality; 67 Dubai Frame/Dubai Municipality; 68l Urbanmyth/Alamy Stock Photo; 68/9 Gavin Hellier/Alamy Stock Photo; 70-73t AA/C Sawyer; 70bl Ayyam Gallery; 70br Dubai Opera; 71bl AA/C Sawyer; 71br Iain Masterton/Alamy Stock Photo; 72bl Iain Masterton/Alamy Stock Photo; 72br Agencja Fotograficzna Caro/Alamy Stock Photo; 73bl James Sullivan/Alamy Stock Photo; 74-75t AA/C Sawyer; 76-78t Level 43 Bar; 78c AA/C Sawyer; 79-80t AA/C Sawyer; 81 AA/C Sawyer; 84tl Courtesy of Atlantis The Palm, Dubai; 84cl Courtesy of Atlantis The Palm, Dubai; 84r Courtesy of Atlantis The Palm, Dubai; 85 Courtesy of Atlantis The Palm, Dubai; 86l Jumeirah.com; 86r AA/C Sawyer; 87 Meraas.com; 88l Keith Erskine/Alamy Stock Photo; 88/9 Robert Harding World Imagery/Alamy Stock Photo; 89cr AA/C Sawyer; 89tr AA/C Sawyer; 90l Madinat Jumeriah; 90r AA/C Sawyer; 91l AA/C Sawyer; 91c AA/C Sawyer; 91r AA/C Sawyer; 92–94t AA/C Sawyer; 92 Tibor Bognar/Alamy Stock Photo; 93bl Robert Harding World Imagery/Alamy Stock Photo; 93br Asia Photopress/Alamy Stock Photo; 94bl Courtesy of Atlantis The Palm; 94br Jumeirah.com; 95 imageBROKER/Alamy Stock Photo; 96t–97t AA/C Sawyer; 97c AA/C Sawyer; 98t AA/C Sawyer; 99 AA/C Sawyer; 102l AA/C Sawyer; 102r AA/C Sawyer; 103t Urbanmyth/Alamy Stock Photo; 103bl Oscar Elias/Alamy Stock Photo; 103br IMG Worlds; 104t–105t ARABIA/Balan Madhavan/Alamy Stock Photo; 104bl Llewellyn/Alamy Stock Photo Stock Photo; 104br Rolf Richardson/Alamy Stock Photo Stock Photo; 105bl Martin Abela/Alamy Stock Photo; 105br Hemis/Alamy Stock Photo; 106t AA/C Sawyer; 108t–112t AA/C Sawyer; 108ct Robert Harding Picture Library Ltd/Alamy Stock Photo; 108cb Enigma/Alamy Stock Photo; 108b Robert Harding Picture Library Ltd/Alamy Stock Photo; 114–115 AA/C Sawyer; 116–117 AA/C Sawyer; 118–119 AA/C Sawyer; 120–122 AA/C Sawyer; 124–125 AA/C Sawyer

Every effort has been made to trace the copyright holders, and we apologise in advance for any accidental errors. We would be happy to apply the corrections in the following edition of this publication.